IN MY FATHER'S HOUSE
St Mary-on-the-Quay – Bristol's Oldest Catholic Church

Kenneth Hankins

St Mary-on-the-Quay
Bristol

First published by St Mary-on-the-Quay, Bristol, 1993

Copyright © 1993 Kenneth Hankins

Designed and typeset by Falling Wall Press Ltd, Bristol
Printed and bound in Great Britain by BPCC Wheatons, Exeter
Cover printed by Doveton Press Ltd, Bristol

Cover picture: water-colour by John Hoar

ISBN 0 9522102 0 7 (paper)
ISBN 0 9522102 1 5 (cased)

St Mary-on-the-Quay
The Presbytery, 20 Colston Street, Bristol BS1 5AE, England

*The principal founder of the Catholic mission
in Bristol was the Jesuit priest,
John Scudamore S.J. (1696-1778).
This book is dedicated to his memory.*

Contents

Illustrations

Cover: 150th anniversary water-colour by John Hoar

Acknowledgements

I have frequently made use of the Jesuit Archives at Mount Street, London, and I am grateful to the Archivist, the Reverend T.G. Holt S.J., for his unfailing help and courtesy.

I am grateful to Bishop Alexander for allowing me to consult the Clifton Diocesan Archives at his residence, St Ambrose. I wish to thank the Reverend Dr J.A. Harding, the Diocesan Archivist, for arranging this for me and for giving me permission to study the Diocesan Archives kept at the Bristol Record Office. Fr Harding has also given me many useful notes covering the period of this history.

Dr John Cashman, the Assistant Diocesan Archivist, has guided me through the archives at St Ambrose and has always been most generous with his help.

I am grateful to the Abbot and to the Librarian, Dom Daniel Rees, for permitting me to use the splendid library at Downside Abbey.

Miss Pamela Gilbert, in the course of her own researches, has given me many useful newspaper references which I might otherwise have missed.

The staff at the Bristol Record Office have always been most helpful and efficient.

The reminiscences of Mrs Mary Harding which appear in this book were kindly provided for me by her daughter, Mrs Mary Brain, who had previously written them for St Mary's Parish Magazine. Historians of St Mary-on-the-Quay will always be indebted to Philip Golden for his editorship of the magazine over 34 years.

Sister M. Cecilia of the Convent of Mercy in Bristol has helped me with information about her Order, the Sisters of Mercy, who have had a long association with St Mary-on-the-Quay through their teaching and service to the poor.

Miss Sue Caple, William Joll and Michael Ray have been most helpful. They have supplied me with much information and answered my queries and I am grateful to them.

Finally I wish to thank the Reverend Claudio Rossi S.J., the Superior and Parish Priest at St Mary-on-the-Quay. It was at his suggestion that I undertook this history, to mark the 150th anniversary of the church, and I am grateful for his encouragement, advice and support.

Kenneth Hankins
Bristol, June 1993

Preface

St Mary-on-the-Quay is central to the history of the Catholic Church in Bristol. It is fascinating to look back over this period and to see how St Mary's takes us back to the time before the Diocese of Clifton came into being. It is interesting to follow the story of a church in central Bristol from 1843 to the present day. On account of its prominent position St Mary's has always had a high profile. It has also had many friends and supporters.

It was a sad day in my life when I had to go to St Mary's and announce at all the Masses that St Mary's would have to close because there was no possibility of raising the funds necessary to repair the roof. Fortunately, I proved to be a false prophet and through the great generosity of the Jesuits and parishioners the church was saved!

There is much information in this book to interest friends of St Mary's, for example, the fact that in the 1850s St Mary's mission covered the area from the top of Park Street to Keynsham or that during the General Mission in 1903 the church was packed every night for the whole fortnight and on the final evening the colonnade and the street in front were thronged.

A book like this is an excellent way of celebrating 150 years in the history of St Mary's. It is a way of paying tribute to those who played a special part in the life and work of the parish whilst not forgetting the many thousands for whom this church was their spiritual home.

+ Mervyn Alexander
Bishop of Clifton

St Joseph's Chapel, in Trenchard Street, behind the Colston Hall. It was the first Catholic church to be built in Bristol since the Reformation. Part of the presbytery can be seen to the right. The buildings have now been developed for housing, but the church façade remains. (Downside Abbey Library)

CHAPTER 1

The New Church
and St James's Back

In 1792, two years after the opening of St Joseph's Chapel in Trenchard Street – the first Catholic church to be built in Bristol since the Reformation – an event occurred in Scotland that was to have a place in the history of the Catholic Church in Bristol.

On the Scottish side of the Solway Firth, not far from Gretna Green (where runaway lovers from England made their vows), there lies the town of Annan; to the west the landscape is one of woods and farmland, while from the Southern Uplands waters gather and run through Annandale towards the sea. It was here, in the small town at the mouth of the river in the closing years of the century, that Edward Irving was born.

After graduating at Edinburgh he studied Presbyterian theology part-time and became an assistant at St John's parish, Glasgow, before moving to London in 1822. He was a powerful preacher and his ability to attract followers showed in the congregations that filled his chapel, but he was a controversial figure, and was eventually dismissed by the London Presbytery and his writings censured by the Presbyterian General Assembly.

One of the most influential forces at work on him was, strangely enough, the writings of the Spanish ex-Jesuit Lacunza, who was in his turn censured by his own brethren and the Holy Office. Lacunza spoke of signs of the Second Coming of Christ and Irving himself became convinced that Christ would return in 1864. Although the Annan Presbytery rejected him, he was admitted deacon in the emerging Catholic Apostolic Church, but he was disappointed with his lowly position in the hierarchy and died, disillusioned, at the early age of 42.

Gradually the Catholic Apostolic Church, or Irvingites as they were known, distanced themselves from the Presbyterian origins of their founder and developed more along High Anglican and Roman Catholic lines. In Bristol a pious and enthusiastic congregation determined to build a new church.[1] *Felix Farley's Journal* of October 21, 1837 reported:

> We have been given to understand that the followers of the late Rev. Mr Irving have purchased a piece of ground under the Bank, as it is called, for the erection of The Church. There will be an extensive frontage, as it includes the Star public house, and goes towards the Drawbridge a considerable distance. It will also run backwards into Host Street, where there will also be a front entrance. For the clearance of the space a good many old, wretched houses will be demolished.

The Irvingites commissioned as their architect a local man, Richard Shackleton Pope, who had a practice in Corn Street. His colleagues were at one in their opinion of him – they all heartily disliked him. His quick temper did not endear him to them and they suspected that at times he was less than scrupulous in the use of his position as a district surveyor. But he was an architect of gifts and achievements, who in his lifetime designed over 200 buildings. He had a special liking for the Grecian temple form, a style no longer quite so fashionable in Europe, but one which had still not lost its appeal. The nineteenth century, with its growth in urban population, was to be a great age of church-building; many of Bristol's churches date from this period. In 1837 the first stone of Pope's new building was laid, and with its completion in 1840 Richard Shackleton Pope gave the centre of Bristol a noble landmark with his new church on the Quay.[2]

The Irvingites, rightly proud of their handsome building (they had purchased for it the Corinthian screen from the renovated Bristol Cathedral) were, however, not long in possession of it. They had overreached themselves and, their numbers declining, were unable to maintain it. After three years they were advertising it for sale, the auctioneer's notice giving its measurements as 92 feet long, 42 feet broad, and 70 feet in the transepts. It was, the notice continued, heated with warm air and lighted with gas.

The Rev. Patrick O'Farrell, who had been a priest at St Joseph's since 1830, seized the opportunity to acquire this fine new church for the growing Catholic population of the city. It required only an altar and organ, and a slight adaptation of the benches, to be ready for service. There was also a small chapel capable of holding about a hundred people, and other rooms. It had cost the Irvingites £15,000: Fr O'Farrell bought it for the diocese for £5,000.

Patrick O'Farrell, a Franciscan friar, was born in Bristol on November 21, 1796 and was baptized at St Joseph's on December 23 by the Jesuit, Robert Plowden, its first priest. After the Jesuits left the city in 1830, Fr O'Farrell served at St Joseph's with Francis Edgeworth, and both distinguished themselves in helping to restore calm during the 'No Popery' riots of November 1831. Now Fr O'Farrell became the first incumbent of St Mary's.

On Sunday, July 5, 1843, Bishop Baines, although in poor health, travelled from Bath on the new Great Western Railway (which had reached Bristol just two years earlier) to dedicate the church – The Church of the Immaculate Conception of the Blessed Virgin Mary on the Quay.[3] The Bishop, an admirer of the Grecian style and conscious of the benefits a city-centre church would bring at a time when the progress of the new cathedral in Clifton was faltering, had supported Fr O'Farrell in his venture, though confessing himself perplexed as to how it would be paid for.

Admission to the ceremony of the opening was by ticket, and at 11 o'clock the procession entered by the vestry on the east side of the altar. The *Bristol Mercury* was at pains to give precise details, wishing to convey the splendour of the occasion:

The Sub-Deacon, Rev. H. Astropp, habited in his gorgeous vestments of cloth-of-gold, with a richly-embroidered stole, bearing a cross of silver gilt.
    Four torch-bearers with lighted tapers.
    Four acolytes.
    The thurifer with the incense.
    The Bishop's attendants.
    The Rev. J. Bonomi, of Prior Park College, who was the conductor of the ceremonies within the altar.
    Between thirty and forty priests, including some monks from Downside Abbey,[4] in their robes, walking two by two.

Rev. Dr Brindle, Vice-Rector of Prior Park College, and
Vicar-General of the Western District.

An attendant bearing the Bishop's crozier of silver,
richly jewelled.

An attendant bearing the Bishop's mitre.

The Deacon, Rev. H. Woolet, in vestments of
cloth-of-gold.

The Rev. Patrick O'Farrell, Officiating High Priest, also
habited in vestments of cloth-of-gold, with an elaborately
embroidered stole and maniple.

Rev. Mr Rooker, officiating as conductor of the
ceremonies within the chapel.

During the time the procession moved slowly along the
east and centre aisles of the church, the rich tones of the
new and powerful organ, by Bishop, added to the solemnity
of the scene. On arriving at the front of the altar, the Rt
Rev. Dr Baines, Bishop of Siga, habited in his purple cope,
with hood of ermine, entered the chapel from the west
vestry, attended by his Chaplains, Rev. Mr Sheehy and the
Rev. J. Illingworth, President of St Peter's College at Prior
Park, and the Rev. Thomas Shattock, President of St Paul's
College at Prior Park. The Chaplains and the assistant
priests were habited in Dalmatic robes of silver dalina,
richly embroidered with gold.

The Bishop and the priests, having ranged themselves in
front and by the sides of the altar, knelt down and the Rev.
P. O'Farrell sang, in English, a prayer from the Breviary,
'Let us adore the God of Glory', the music being composed
by Manners of Bath. The choral responses were executed by
the choir... High Mass, coram Pontifice, was then
commenced by the High Priest [Fr O'Farrell], assisted by
the Rev. Deacon and the Rev. Sub-Deacon. The Bishop,
having taken his seat under a canopy on the West side of
the altar, was unrobed of his cope and habited in far more
gorgeous vestments, his mitre, richly jewelled, being placed
on his head.

The Mass was celebrated according to the form always
used on such occasions. After the 'Agnus Dei' had been
sung, the 'Pax' or 'Kiss of Peace' was given by the Bishop

to his assistant-priests and chaplains, and then by the priests to each other. The music of the service was by Haydn, it being his Mass No.2, and it was effectively performed by the choir which had been augmented for the occasion. Signor Guiscard of London presided at the organ.

The soloists were from Bristol, Bath and London. Bishop Baines took as the theme for his sermon 'The Four Marks of the True Church'.

... At the conclusion of the Mass, the Bishop and the priests surrounded the altar and chanted the 'Te Deum', after which the procession was reformed and preceded His Lordship, habited in Episcopal Vestments, bearing his crozier and wearing his mitre and jewels, around the aisles to the east vestry. The ceremony of the opening being thus concluded, the company left the church.

After the service, the choir partook of a collation at the Royal Western Hotel, which was liberally provided by the resident priests.

The ceremony lasted until 2 p.m.; over the entrance to the sacristy an inscription today commemorates the occasion. "After the service," wrote Dr Brindle, the Vicar-General, "the poor, with whom the Bishop was a special favourite, crowded upon him and were seen to kiss the hem of his cappa magna as he passed." It may be observed here that Dr Brindle, who had once been a monk at Ampleforth, was mainly responsible, three years later, for establishing the Convent of the Sisters of Mercy in Dighton Street, Bristol; for nearly 50 years the Sisters taught in the schools of St Mary-on-the-Quay and won the esteem of all who saw their service and devotion to the poor.

On returning to Prior Park the Bishop felt unwell and rested, but insisted later on joining a reception of priests before finally retiring to bed. The dedication of St Mary-on-the-Quay was the last public duty he performed, for on entering his bedroom at 7 o'clock the next morning his manservant found him dead: he was 57 years of age.

1843 was the year in which the Prince Consort came to Bristol
and, while some 30,000 people watched from Brandon Hill,
launched the S.S. Great Britain, the largest ship afloat. It was also
the year in which for another great project the money ran out:
work on the Clifton Suspension Bridge ceased and for the next 20
years the towers either side of the gorge stood detached and
deprived of purpose, 'follies' as they came to be known. And it
was also the year in which the Poet Laureate, Robert Southey,
died; he had been born 69 years earlier, barely a stone's throw
from the site of St Mary-on-the-Quay.

St Mary's had an imposing position in the centre of Bristol.
Situated on Under the Bank, as Colston Avenue was called in
those days, it rose above two-storeyed sixteenth and seventeenth
century gabled dwellings and the more recent Georgian buildings
adjacent to it. To the rear it was bordered by Host Street,[5] a
narrow cobbled lane that earlier Catholics would have known as
Horse Street. Half-way along its line of gabled buildings, most
still with iron casements on the upper floors, a wall lantern
signified a welcome to the Flitch of Bacon Tavern.

It was, of course, a waterside area, busy in commerce and
trade. William Wright, wine and brandy merchants, had premises
a few yards from the church, as did Pickford and Co., Severn
Carriers, who had only been there a year but were well thought
of by their customers. The Monmouthshire Coal Company did
business near by.

Mass-goers were able to note some useful addresses: John
Clift, hair cutter and perfumer, was at No.14, and John Griffiths,
a plumber, was recommended for his water closets. And William
Cornish, who was a cabinet-maker by trade, finding that one skill
leads to another and perhaps encouraged by the presence of a
church close at hand, declared himself an undertaker as well. But
service to man can take many forms and at the Artichoke Tavern
Robert Hardcastle acted as host, while further on, amongst the
agents and wharfingers, lived Mr C. Pache, incongruous but
unabashed, as Ornithologist.

Across the narrow road from the steps of St Mary's, bollards
marked the quayside and the Frome flowed, still an open river, its
waters carrying barges and small vessels. To the left towards
Broadmead was the Stone Bridge, and to the right the

Drawbridge, beyond which could be seen the rigging of the tall ships, so that in the very heart of the city, amidst its streets and walls, dwellings and warehouses, lived the sights and echoes of the sea.

It was a scene that had intrigued visitors through the ages. In the eighteenth century the great poet, Alexander Pope, recalled it in a letter to a friend: "From thence you come to a key along the old wall, with houses on both sides, and in the middle of the street as far as you can see, hundreds of ships, their masts as thick as they can stand by one another, which is the oddest and most surprising sight imaginable ... A long street full of ships in the middle, with houses on each side, looks like a dream."

But the river that flowed past St Mary's linked the city's Catholics with a more significant moment in their history. A few hundred yards away, where upstream the waters narrowed through Lewins Mead, they suddenly swung right and parallel to a centuries-old street called St James's Back, now completely changed and known as Silver Street. A hundred years earlier, at a time when Alexander Pope was making a second visit to the city, a Jesuit Priest, John Scudamore, was given permission to set up his chapel there, primarily because the authorities had promised freedom of worship to Catholic artisans from France and Flanders whose skills, particularly in brass-making, were needed for local industry. Harsh penal laws against Catholics were still on the Statute-book, but this good priest faithfully served the Catholics of Bristol for over 30 years, and so established the Bristol mission within the city boundaries where previously there had been none since the Reformation.

St James's Back was a straight, narrow street intersecting Broadmead, now Bristol's busiest shopping centre. What remains of it today takes its name (Silver Street) from a small, adjacent road that no longer exists. William Worcester, the first of modern English antiquarians, and reputedly the first man to translate Cicero into English, was born in St James's Back (or Bec as he called it) in 1415, an indication of how old the street was even in the eighteenth century. It contained some of the oldest houses in the city – gabled buildings suggesting medieval and Elizabethan times, cluttered with the overhanging signs of numerous trades, often a hazard to passing traffic.

Food and drink could readily be bought on the Back. At one
time customers had the choice of six butchers and a tripe shop,
and those in search of ale and company could, with a few pence
in their pocket, frequent the Sugar Loaf, or one of the other
taverns in the narrow thoroughfare – the Crown and Cushion, the
Three Tuns, the Star, the White Hart, or Jack Newbery.
Elsewhere in the street four tailors vied for custom. The sign of
a bible and sun hung over the premises of Mr Crowe and Thomas
Daniels – their bookshops long established in St James's Back.
The proximity of so many trades in one street suggests that no
one really flourished or expected to; the poor would doubtless be
very poor.

Two other buildings helped to establish the character of St
James's Back: there was a Gift House and a Poor House. The
former was occupied by four women and two men who depended
on such gifts as 25p each, received every quarter day from the
churchwardens. In the Poor House an old man and his wife lived
in one apartment and received between them 10p a week from the
churchwardens and, from time to time, such articles as a coat or
shirt. A woman and her daughter were in another apartment and,
for both of them, received just over 7p weekly, again from the
churchwardens of St James's parish.

The place available for John Scudamore to set up his chapel
was a wretched enough building, no more than the upper floor of
a kind of warehouse, which could accommodate between 60 and
80 worshippers. For this the Jesuits paid the owner, Richard
Webb, rent of £11 a year; for the purposes of the Poor Law it
was rated at just 5p.[6] The building was set back in a cheerless
courtyard, towards one end of the street, which, perhaps
inevitably, came to be known as Chapel Court. During the dark
evenings no street lamp cast its light at the entrance; indeed there
was not one to be seen the length of the street. But the residents
on St James's Back did not feel particularly hard done by, for in
truth there was not one street light in the whole parish.

Although this old chapel served Bristol's Catholics for some
half century, maps never showed its position. As far as the civic
authorities were concerned, it was a private mass-house
accommodated in part of a building erected for other purposes;
there was, accordingly, no reason to identify such a place

publicly. But it is still possible to establish its location if we can trace the old building's subsequent history, and if there is anything that would then entitle it to be identified on future maps. It was bought by the religious followers of the Swedish philosopher and scientist, Emanuel Swedenborg, who, after his conversion in 1743 (about the time John Scudamore set up his chapel), had believed himself to be in constant communication with spirits who dictated to him revelations of the next world. The Swedenborgians enlarged the building, giving it a gallery and installing an organ; its size and character were now such that as a church – the New Jerusalem Church – it could be marked officially on city maps. Find the New Jerusalem Church and we have the site of Father Scudamore's historic chapel – always providing it is in St James's Back! Mathews's plan of the city for 1794 shows not only the new Catholic Chapel of St Joseph's, in Trenchard Lane, but also the New Jerusalem Church standing, as we would hope, in St James's Back.

The present writer estimates the site to be about 40 yards along today's Silver Street, from the St James's end, and to be roughly in line with Wesley's Room across the way, though a little nearer the Horsefair than the latter. At the time of this being written the site is occupied by part of the premises of a book shop. Subsequently the New Jerusalem Church building became used as a ragged school, run by the Church of England.

The value to the Catholics of Bristol of John Scudamore's chapel was immeasurable, for in those difficult times, though ignored on the maps of the city and allowed only on sufferance, it maintained its presence and so gave impetus to the Catholic cause. Thus it prefigured the historic church of St Joseph which the Jesuits were to build in Trenchard Street, and the church of St Mary-on-the-Quay, which they were later to own and serve.

NOTES

1. In the meantime they had a place of worship in Lower Montague Street. While they were in their new church the Irvingites held Divine Service every day at 6 a.m. and 5 p.m. On Sundays services were at 10 a.m. and 2 p.m. After selling the

building they moved to the Iron Church, Upper Berkeley Place, Clifton.

The Roman Catholic church in Frome (vacated in 1927) was also purchased from the Irvingites.

2. It is possible that Pope drew inspiration from the choragic Monument of Lysicrates, or Lamp of Diogenes, erected in Athens in 334 B.C.; it had six Corinthian columns. The façade of St Pancras Church, London (1819-1822) is similar to St Mary's. Bryan Little is precise: "The plan, of a temple set seemingly astride a lateral building which seems to run through it, has its first appearance in Britain in Thomas Hamilton's Royal High School, Edinburgh (1829) and was taken seriously by the Scottish architects." *Bristol – an architectural history* by Andor Gomme, Michael Jenner, Bryan Little, 1979, p.240.

3. "The Church was originally dedicated to the B.V. Mary, but as this was transferred to another Church on the Quay, our Church is called St Joseph's." *Clifton Visitation Papers (St Joseph's) 1858-59*, Bristol Record Office.

4. Downside Abbey: then known as Downside College, Bath.

5. Host Street was called Horstrete by William Worcester in 1460. This becomes Horse Street on Mathews's plan of the city in 1794, and Host Street by the time of Chilcott's map of 1838. It was one of the first streets in Bristol to be paved, in 1490.

Host Street was named as one of the chief places where Catholics lived. *Clifton Visitation Papers (St Joseph's) 1858-59*, Bristol Record Office.

6. For the most part, money is expressed in this book in today's terms, although, of course, values are different. "Richard Webbe" is the spelling to be found in the Jesuit Archives in London, and the sum mentioned in connection with the Poor Law, one shilling.

"In March of 1788 the foundations of the chapel and house in Trenchard Street were begun and St Joseph's Chapel itself was opened on Sunday, June 27th, 1790. The six months' warning for giving up the tenement of St James' Back, rented for £11 per annum, had just expired." *Letters & Notices*, Vol.26, Jesuit Archives, London.

CHAPTER 2

Early Difficulties at St Mary's

At the time of the opening of St Mary's, the two Catholic priests in the city, Fr Edgeworth and Fr O'Farrell, were numbered among Bristol's 33 Dissenting ministers; the Established Church had around 70 clergy.

There can be no doubt that some Protestants in the city were well disposed towards the Catholics. When he addressed the congregation at St Joseph's at the opening of the chapel in 1790, Fr Plowden was conscious of this and that they had contributed funds towards the building of the church, and he urged his fellow Catholics to be "mindful of, and pray for the welfare of those who are non-Catholics." That there were such present in his audience "must," he said, "make the day the more joyful and more glorious, in which the brotherhood and friendship are renewed; and the more so, the longer time has passed since we were seen together under the same roof." And as if in reassurance to Catholics and Protestants alike, he added that Catholics should hold firmly to the maxims of their religion "as there is not a tenet, or item in it, if duly understood that can give the smallest occasion of suspicion or offence to any man."

But in 1843 that was not how all Protestants in Bristol saw things: there were some associations active against the Catholic cause. Of the 28 'Societies for the Promotion of Christianity' in the city, the 'Bristol Protestant Association', for instance, existed for the purpose of "disseminating knowledge of the principles and practices of the Church of Rome" (i.e. for discrediting it). It had as its patron no less a figure than the Duke of Beaufort; and P.W.S. Miles, one of the city's two Members of Parliament, was vice-president. The society met at 8 Nelson Street, at the premises of Daniel Vickery, a bookseller.

Then there was an organisation bizarrely calling itself 'Bristol and Clifton Association for promoting the Moral and Religious Improvement of Ireland', which was run by two English clergymen. That, too, met at Daniel Vickery's shop in Nelson Street.

The shop in Nelson Street was indeed a busy place. Under the listings of "Institutions for Charitable Purposes" for 1843 was one headed "Penitentiary or Magdalene House": "This valuable institution, established in 1800, receives those unhappy females who have strayed from the paths of virtue, and have a desire to recover their character. They are employed in needle-work etc. till they are deemed worthy to be placed in situations, or restored to their friends." The Assistant Secretary to this body? The earnest bookseller of Nelson Street – Daniel Vickery.

From time to time Bristol's newspapers, as though by way of salutary warning, would alert their readers to the dangers, as they saw it, of Rome. A year after the dedication of St Mary's, almost to the day, *Felix Farley's Bristol Journal*, under the heading "Popery in the Nineteenth Century", warned its Protestant readers not to be betrayed into departure from their faith by "the gorgeous ceremonial, the fascinating music, and above all, the gentle aspect it [Popery] wears in Protestant England. Here it puts forth only a velvet paw; history tells us how deadly is its clutch."

On Sunday, April 19, 1846, Fr O'Farrell denounced *Felix Farley's Journal* from the pulpit of St Mary's for reporting that "some of the absurdities of Popery," as the newspaper had put it, were being introduced into Bristol. His rebuke brought a sharp retort from the *Journal* the following week: "We shall continue to protest against the soul-destroying system of Rome – the most deadly heresy that ever impeded the progress of the religion of Christ."

The Oxford Movement[1] of the 1830s within the Anglican Church, and John Henry Newman's conversion to Rome in 1845, had made many Protestants of the time particularly sensitive of Catholic influence and the need to be vigilant against what they considered to be its pernicious effect.

Aware, then, of hostile sentiment from some quarters and the possibility, even at that time, of it being translated into political action, it was not unusual at Parliamentary elections for Catholics in the city to consult together as a body. A sophisticated judgement was sometimes called for, as *Felix Farley's Journal* seemed to indicate when reporting the hustings of July 1852:

On the Quay. The earliest photograph of St Mary's in the Jesuit Archives. The River Frome, which can be clearly seen, was covered over in 1893; the area eventually became Colston Avenue. (Photo: Jesuit Archives)

We believe we are correct in stating that the advice of the
priests [at a meeting at St Mary-on-the-Quay] was to throw
the influence of the 140 or 150 Roman Catholic votes into
the scale in favour of Mr McGeachy as they would prefer
the open enmity of that gentleman to the dubious coquetries
of Messrs Berkeley and Langton.

But even though some newspapers were, on occasions,
anti-Roman, they reported Catholic news. On November 6 that
year, the *Bristol Journal* carried the following item:

During the past week, for the first time probably since the
Reformation, two Roman Catholic Missionaries (Jesuits we
believe) have preached three times daily to crowded
congregations of all denominations, at various Roman
Catholic chapels in our city. The Roman Catholics assert
that between 40 and 50 conversions have been the fruits of
these missions.

One reader, signing himself "A Clergyman", was sufficiently
agitated by this success to write to the paper urging the
Established Church to be as active in their own cause as the
Jesuits in theirs. This kind of mission was to be a feature of
Catholic life in the city during the years to come, with similar
attendant success.

What did the interior of St Mary's originally look like? We have
this eyewitness account from the *Bristol Mercury* dated July 8,
1843, a few days after the opening ceremony:

The erection is considered by competent judges to be one of
the purest specimens of Greek architecture in the Kingdom,
and is certainly ranked among the most beautiful edifices in
this city.
    The entrance to the building is by a magnificent portico,
supported by columns upon the plan of one of the most
exquisite models of antiquity, the Diogenes Lantern at
Athens.
    The interior, which is cruciform, contains about 4,000

superficial feet and is capable of containing 600 persons. The sanctuary, which is supported by four elegant Corinthian columns, is situated at the north-west extremity and on its right and left are the statues of Saint Peter and Saint Paul, the former holding the keys, the latter holding the sword. Over the altar is fixed a crucifix, with the Saviour in burnished gold, surrounded by a halo, gilt with the same precious metal. On the altar are placed twelve elegantly-chased candle-sticks of silver gilt. The antependium, or drapery, in front, was worked by nuns of the Visitation Convent at Westbury. It is of crimson velvet, richly embroidered with gold. In the centre is a Maltese Cross, and in the side compartments are wreaths of the vine and ears of wheat.

There being no gallery or enclosed pews in the church, its appearance is exceedingly light and lofty, and the novel and chaste character of the gas-fittings harmonises well with the general style of the edifice and produces a *tout ensemble* of extreme architectural beauty.

It is interesting to note that, although there was at that time no gallery, the church could seat 600 people; today there are probably not more than three churches in the diocese with this capacity.[2]

St Mary's had cost £5,000. The arrangement had been for £500 to be paid on June 1, 1843, £2,000 at the beginning of September, and the rest to remain on mortgage. The repayment of the money was to be a troublesome burden to Fr O'Farrell for years to come. One of his first moves was to issue a passionate appeal to the readership of the Catholic national magazine, *The Tablet*, but it seems no capital sum was forthcoming, for in 1903 an elderly parishioner looking back on those days remarked: "It must have been borrowed for we were always collecting to pay the interest."

At first Fr O'Farrell entertained the idea of putting into practice a scheme that was not unknown abroad, in churches in France, for instance, but caused unease amongst English Catholics: he proposed charging for admission to St Mary's. A placard on the walls of the church stated:

As all previous arrangements made for the admission of the
public into the Chapel were found inefficient, the charge for
admission will be as follows, viz. Reserved seats, morning
1s. evening, 6d.; Middle seats, morning 6d., evening 3d.;
Lower seats 3d., evening the same; entrance by side doors
to the open space, 1d.; no free sittings.

'Seat rents' were another source of income for any church
struggling to pay its way, and they continued in some form at St
Mary's and other churches (e.g. the Pro-Cathedral) into the next
century.

Two years later Fr O'Farrell launched another scheme. On
Wednesday, October 15, 1845, he called a public meeting at St
Mary's Church of the Catholics of Bristol and Clifton, at which
it was agreed that "the principal purpose of the future Collections
be the formation of a sinking-fund for paying off the purchase
money of the Church of St Mary's, on the Quay, Bristol; and St
Augustine's Chapel, Clifton."

By 1847 there was the possibility of another, more radical,
resolution of St Mary's financial problems. Could the Society of
Jesus be persuaded to take over the church and its debts? The
Jesuits, and their supporters in the city, had no doubt of their
right to return to Bristol and the mission they had founded, but
did St Mary's come within their plans? There was a busy
correspondence between Bishop Ullathorne and the Provincial,[3]
Fr Randal Lythgoe, and between Fr Lythgoe and Fr O'Farrell.

What was being proposed? The Jesuits sought clarification, for
"I am sure," the Provincial wrote to Fr O'Farrell, "that no one is
more anxious than yourself that union should be restored amongst
the Catholics of Bristol." Fr O' Farrell suggested, with the
Bishop's approval, that St Joseph's should be turned into schools
and that the Society should take over St Mary's with its debts,
"and that immediately, in order to prevent accumulation of debt."
As for himself, Fr O'Farrell said, "I can readily consent to yield
my position in order to promote the harmonious working of the
mission."

It was May 1847. The plan was taking shape and the Bishop
was able to tell the Provincial the boundaries he proposed for the
parish: Clifton on the west, Stokes Croft on the east, and Bristol

Bridge and the Floating Harbour on the south. To the north, he wrote, the parish would extend "indefinitely towards the Downs where it is stopped by Westbury." He left the Provincial to ponder an interesting – and telling – afterthought, added by way of postscript: "We are celebrating the month of May in St Mary's and the Church is crowded every night."

The Provincial expressed his willingness to take over St Mary's and the debt of £5,000, but intended to proceed cautiously. He informed Dr Ullathorne that he was instructing his architect to report on the state of the building, and his solicitor to examine the title-deed.

What was to follow dismayed the Bishop. In August Fr Lythgoe wrote to say he was awaiting the lawyer's report, but "from what I have heard so far I fear that the Title is such that I cannot with safety move to deal with it." September brought a further blow. Not only was there, as expected, an unfavourable report on the tenure of St Mary's, but the architect's comments on the state of the building led Fr Lythgoe to remark to the Bishop that a "very great risk is thought likely to attend the keeping of St Mary's by whomsoever it is held." He accordingly declined his lordship's offer.

The Bishop, alarmed by this intelligence, following so soon on his own lawyer's advice that the finances of St Mary's had to be put on a sound footing – and that without delay – turned his attention to the person at the centre of these concerns – if not, indeed, the cause! Had Fr O'Farrell shown enough economic foresight? Dr Ullathorne expressed himself surprised, moreover, that an earlier meeting at St Mary's to discuss their affairs had been so poorly attended and by so "few influential men." He thought he could see the reason. Fr O'Farrell would secure more support, he suggested, if only he showed "a little of that attention and civility and those *bienséances* which become such occasions." The Bishop pursued the point: "The old want of confidence on the part of numbers of Bristol Catholics, [is] entirely, I believe, arising from a want of a little more conciliation of manner towards those who naturally take their own little views." Thinking to tap fresh resources he proposed the formation of a large committee from the St Mary's congregation to assist their priest.

Piqued by these comments, Fr O'Farrell wrote a courteous but

spirited reply defending himself, suggesting that perhaps he had
the opportunity of knowing the Catholics of Bristol better than his
lordship. But the management committee was formed and on
March 31, 1848 made its first report. The debt had been reduced
to £4,804. Welcome news, and the situation would have been
better still but "many Catholics who attend the services of the
Church do not seem to feel the obligation of contributing to its
resources, since they continually and from time to time refuse to
make their offering on Sundays."

In the following example[4] for September, 1848, we are able to
see St Mary's receipts for a month. The weekly "Collection"
referred to was the proceeds of the scheme whereby the parish
was divided into districts with collectors calling on "regular"
contributors; the church committee hoped eventually to divide
the town into 40 districts, each district being expected to
contribute ten shillings (50p) weekly. The committee also
encouraged people who could afford it "to take a sitting" (the
item "Seat Rents"):

Sept.	4	Week's Collection	£4 .14 .11
	3	.. Offertory	4 . 4 . 9
	11	.. Collection	2 . 6 . 5
	10	.. Offertory	3 . 0 . 9
	18	.. Collection	4 .11 . 3
	17	.. Offertory	4 . 2 .11
		Seat Rents	3 . 9 . 9
	25	.. Collection	5 . 0 . 0
	24	.. Offertory	3 . 9 . 2
			34 .19 . 1

Fr O'Farrell tackled the problem yet again in 1849, upon the
arrival of the new bishop. Together with his committee, and with
the approbation of Bishop Hendren, he explored the mode of
redeeming the mortgage on the Church by means of purchasing
shares in an Investment Society:

The good work of ensuring the church would therefore be
effected, if 40 persons could be found, who would consent
to pay £5 per annum for 13 years; because in that period,

after deductions of £2 7s. 0d. per share for expenses of administration, the sum of £3,854 4s. would be realized, the mortgage being £3,900.

Until Fr O'Farrell's retirement from St Mary's in 1857, raising money to pay off the debt was a constant worry and a task that continually engaged his attention.

NOTES

1. A movement initiated in 1833 within the Church of England which emphasised the 'Catholic' nature of the Anglican Church. Its most famous member was John Henry Newman (1801-90) who, in 1841, published a tract on the compatibility of the Thirty-nine Articles with Roman Catholic theology. In 1845 he joined the Church of Rome and was created Cardinal in 1879.
2. Excluding those churches served by Religious there are three churches in the diocese of Clifton with a normal seating capacity of 600 or more – Bristol Polish Church (650), Cheltenham St Thomas More (600), Bristol Cathedral (800). *Diocese of Clifton Working Party on Deployment of Clergy*, Appendix 1.
3. For administrative purposes the Society of Jesus is divided into Provinces. The English Province includes Scotland and Wales. "The Superior of each Province (known as the 'Provincial') is appointed by the General. His term of office usually lasts not more than six years. Under the General he has overall responsibilty and authority within his Province for the Jesuits and their apostolate." *The Jesuits in England* by Francis Edwards S.J., 1985.
4. *Letters and Papers 1837-49*, Clifton Diocesan Archives, 35721, Bristol Record Office.

Old houses in the Pithay, a turning off St James's Back where the Catholics of Bristol went to Mass in the eighteenth century. In the nineteenth century many Catholics who worshipped at St Mary's lived in this area. (Photo: Martyn Jetzer)

CHAPTER 3

St Mary's Schools

Throughout the Church's history, religious institutions have been centres of learning and providers of education. Before the advent of state education in this country in the latter part of the nineteenth century, and indeed beyond, society owed a great debt to the work of the many church schools throughout the land.

Direct state intervention in education had always been hesitant and reluctant until the government concerned itself with elementary education in 1833, by allotting money to voluntary bodies, and from then on church and state co-operated to provide a form of basic schooling. By the time of the important Education Act of 1870, when Board schools supplemented the numbers of voluntary schools and the authorities were empowered to enforce the attendance at school of children aged between five and 13, 21 of the schools in Bristol owed their origins to the city's churches.

It was Fr Robert Plowden S.J. who established the Catholic Charity School in Bristol when the St Joseph premises in Trenchard Street were built in 1789, and then maintained it with some difficulty at his own expense together with contributions from members of the congregation.

We get some picture of the sums involved and the scale of things from the figures presented to the School Committee in 1823, some eight years after after Fr Plowden had left the city:

Subscriptions and Donations	£76	5	6
Collections	16	11	8
Pence and Admission Money	20	3	6
Chapel Boxes	0	12	7
Interest on Savings' Bank Deposit	3	10	3
Balance, 16 May, 1822	11	8	11
	£128	12	5

From this the Master and Mistress received their salaries and all other expenses were paid, leaving a balance of £38.16.1d. Two years later the School Committee was told:

> Within the last four years, forty-three boys have been branched off, some to trades, and others to useful employments; in general, they wrote useful hands, and were well advanced in cyphering, and their employers have expressed satisfaction as to their conduct; the number of boys in the school is seventy, and girls upwards of fifty.[1]

It seems that 1836 was a difficult year. The master complained that the boys, many of whom were ill-clad and barefoot, could not endure the extreme cold, and coals were fetched from the dwelling house.

The provision of funds for its schools was one of the major concerns of Catholics from the earliest days of St Mary's. In 1843 the Catholic Poor School Committee had been set up to claim the government grant, which contributed half the cost of building schools, but nothing towards running them. The description 'poor schools' continued until 1896 when the word 'Poor' was dropped from the Committee's title.

A leaflet issued by the Bristol Catholic Poor Schools in 1845, under the patronage of the Earl and Countess of Shrewsbury (who had contributed to the building of St Joseph's) appealed to people beyond the precincts of the city for subscriptions and support. It stated that, although the Catholic population numbered several thousands, the great proportion were poor and very few were capable of meeting the necessities of the case. One thousand children required education – 220 were receiving it.

Benevolence was, for good reason, of a practical kind and sometimes from unexpected quarters:

> Also by private subscription of about £13 (more than half of which was contributed by Protestants) 62 of the girls received at Christmas articles of wearing apparel, as an encouragement to good behaviour and punctuality in attending school and divine worship; 26 received a frock, bonnet, shawl, and a pair of boots each, 36 received a shawl and bonnet each, and 24 of them received a pair of

stockings each in addition.[2]

The next year Bishop Ullathorne preached at the chapel of St Joseph on the need to raise money for the Catholic Poor Schools, and on the following Sunday, when addressing the congregation at St Mary-on-the-Quay, stressed the paramount Christian duty of educating the poor.

In the years ahead the cost of maintaining the schools in Bristol exceeded income and the committee acknowledged "with gratitude the contributions of many liberal Protestants." They considered that the numbers and destitution of the Catholic poor in the city probably exceeded, comparatively, those of any large town in England.

In 1852 a schoolroom was opened at St Mary's for the boys, but the girls still had to go to the school at Clifton run by the Sisters of Penance. Education was not then compulsory and the boys' attendance ranged from 50 to 70, although 120 were of school age. Parents were expected to pay a penny a week towards their child's education – but many did not.

The end of 1858 saw the completion of the first year of the amalgamation of the boys' schools of St Joseph and St Mary. What did Her Majesty's Inspector think of their work? "It is satisfactory to me to report that this school, which was formerly in a comparatively inefficient state, is now conducted under a zealous and capable teacher. Reading, Writing and Spelling, are taught with complete success, while in Grammar and Arithmetic fair progress has been made. The great improvement in the discipline deserves special remark. The school seems to me full of promise." So far, so good – but the management committee added a rider of their own: "Satisfactory as the attendance and conduct of the boys at school have been, their attendance at Mass on Sundays and Holidays of Obligation has been, and continues to be, disproportionately small. The committee earnestly call the attention of parents and guardians to this serious evil." This stricture seems to have yielded fruit because the following year the committee were able to report: "The scholars have not only grown in numbers, but have also improved in their attendance at church and the sacraments."

By the 1860s the average attendance at the boys' school had

risen to 163, and at the girls' school, by then in Dighton Street with the Sisters of Mercy, to 300.

A popular way of raising money for the schools was by means of an evening concert and refreshment – a soirée, to use the parlance of the time. Such an evening was held in the schoolroom at St Mary's on October 27, 1869. The *Western Daily Press* reported that the room was decorated for the occasion with flowers and evergreens, and the concert was preceded by a gathering for tea, which "was very numerously attended." The audience was then entertained by singers and performers at the pianoforte: it all made for a most pleasant evening, and one that was successful too "when regarded in a pecuniary point of view."

St Joseph's Chapel was closed on November 19th, 1871, and after its interior had been transformed it was opened in 1873 as an infant school for poor children and as a meeting room. The Bishop announced the fact in his Pastoral Letter of November 23rd that year: "New and ample accommodation has been provided for the infants of the schools of St Mary's." By the 1880s St Mary's schools for boys and girls were well established, but were again appealing for funds.

Another way in which money was raised was through what St Mary's called, in their publicity leaflets,[3] "The Annual Sermons and Collections for the Schools attached to St Mary's". On the Sunday concerned there would be High Mass and sermon at 11 a.m., and Vespers and sermon at 6.30, probably with a visiting preacher. Sometimes the music, both morning and evening, would be with orchestral accompaniment. "Subscriptions," the leaflets added, "are earnestly solicited." These, together with money raised from entertainments, amounted to about one-fifth of St Mary's school receipts by the end of the century, but it was a struggle to meet expenses and in some years the schools were running at a deficit.

Another information leaflet, headed "Course of Religious Instruction to be followed in the Elementary Schools of the Diocese of Clifton", outlined the syllabus for each standard, starting with the infants, and continuing for standards I, II, III, and IV. Pupils in standard IV were required to know:

By heart: The whole of the Catechism. Correct knowledge

of chief Festivals and Services of the Church, also of the chief Miracles and Parables of Our Lord, and of his Sermon on the Mount. Bible History, down to the building of the Temple of Solomon; with a general knowledge of the Kings, the Prophets, the Captivity of Babylon, and the return to the land of Juda.

There was one matter that was of particular concern to the Catholic authorities in the city at the turn of the century. They felt that many Catholic children were losing their faith through involvement with non-Catholic organisations where, inevitably, there was no Catholic instruction. An incident which took place in July 1894 illustrates they were prepared to stop the drift.

The Children's Help Society had organised a summer camp which some children from St Mary's Schools were attending. After consulting together the headmaster, Mr Harrington, and the parents concerned went to the camp and took their children away. The *Bristol Mercury*, learning of the affair, felt that the Catholics had over-reacted and observed that the children themselves, no doubt puzzled by the whole business, probably felt that their greatest danger lay in missing their camp dinners that day.

Having, as he thought, put the matter into perspective, the writer yet showed himself sensitive to the issues involved:

It is perfectly well known that Catholics do not participate in unsectarian services and cannot take the same view of them as Protestants, while the children would be doing a great wrong if they did not hear Mass on Sunday. It is well known that Catholics consider that they ought to be exempt from School Board rates because they are prepared to educate their children in their own schools, and this action of the Trenchard Street fathers is merely coming into line with the general attitude.

The Catholics tried to keep a careful watch over their children in the city who were in orphanages or living with non-Catholic foster parents, and who were therefore at risk, so it was felt, of losing their faith. Wherever possible the nuns took take care of them, but it was hoped that ultimately the School Committee would provide a suitable house that could be devoted entirely to such children under Catholic care.

At the end of the nineteenth century the number of children on the registers of St Mary's schools were: Boys 135, Girls 133, and Infants 125.[4]

NOTES

1. Documents relating to St Joseph's, Clifton Diocesan Archives, 35721, Bristol Record Office.
2. Report of the Bristol Catholic Poor Schools for 1845, *Papers 1837-49*, Clifton Diocesan Archives, 35721, Bristol Record Office.
3. Leaflets for Sundays May 4, 1884; March 27, 1887; June 16, 1889; May 18, 1890. *Bristol Papers*, Jesuit Archives, London.
4. Report on St Mary's Schools 1897-98, Clifton Diocesan Archives, 35721, Bristol Record Office.

CHAPTER 4

The Catholic Community in the 1840s

When Bishop Baines visited Rome in 1840 (the year in which St Mary's was built) he was able to present statistics to the Pope showing that there were 275 baptisms in Bristol during the previous 12 months and there had been 26 conversions; Easter communicants numbered 2,400.

Sunday services at St Mary's in the months immediately following its opening were at 11 a.m. and 6 p.m. Fr O'Farrell was soon to be joined on the staff by Fr Joseph Prendergast and Fr Edward Cullinan, and in time the number of Masses increased.

Fr Cullinan was assisting, too, in other areas of Bristol's Catholic community. He ministered at Stapleton Workhouse, but not without difficulty, for the management committee would not permit him to leave religious books with the Catholics, on the grounds that 'sectarian' books and tracts were banned from the institution. The Bishop protested on his behalf, but an exchange of letters produced no satisfactory result.

In those early years priests at St Mary's were also helping to establish the Bedminster mission. Fr Cullinam used a room in a house in Somerset Square, just behind St Mary Redcliff, in which to say Mass on Sundays. Then as the congregation increased he rented a large house across the way at 11 Redcliff Parade, and converted the ground floor into a chapel; a few people from St Joseph's and St Mary's would lend support and help with the singing at Mass and Benediction. Amongst these were Jeremiah Maher and his daughters, Jane and Agnes – Jane playing the piano with Agnes standing one side of her and Jeremiah the other. As a young man Jeremiah had sat at the feet of Robert Plowden during his time at St Joseph's and remained a fierce champion of the redoutable priest, corresponding with him until his death; his family had a great admiration for the Society of Jesus and a commitment to its cause.

By 1863 it was necessary for the Bedminster mission to move

again, this time to a purpose-built chapel, Holy Cross, on the corner of Charlotte Street and East Street. During this period priests of the Pro-Cathedral assumed responsibilty for the Mission.

The numbers of Irish, driven, over the years, by poverty and famine to attempt a new life abroad, were growing in the English towns and cities and such great western seaports as Liverpool and Bristol. In the St Mary's register of Baptisms for 1843, the first year of the church's opening, the frequency of such names as Murphy, Regan, Leahy, O'Connor, Lynch, Brennan, Delaney, Casey, Boyle, Donovan and Fitzgerald, reflected the strong Irish presence in the city. The church inevitably became a focal point for associations such as the Hibernian Society, a benefit society established for the Irish poor in the city. On Whit-Mondays the members would process through the streets, carrying their banners and headed by a band, and then assemble at St Mary's where they would be addressed by Fr O'Farrell.

In those days, while Fr Cullinan was still at St Joseph's, there was a simplicity with which arrangements between the two churches could be made. If necessary, Fr O'Farrell would go up to the altar in the Trenchard Street chapel to possess himself of the chalice for use at Mass in St Mary's.

About this time the merchants, attorneys, and gentlefolk in the elegant buildings lining fashionable Queen Square, restored after the destruction of the 1831 riots, were intrigued to learn that the house across the way had become, at least for the time being, a convent of Catholic nuns. For 300 years such convents had not been seen in Bristol until the Sisters of Mercy arrived in Dighton Street; now Bishop Ullathorne had persuaded the Dominican Order of the Sisters of Penance to establish a community in the city, and they took up residence in the square while awaiting completion of their new building in Clifton. The congregation of St. Mary-on-the-Quay were soon aware of their new neighbours; on two occasions in 1847 the Bishop conducted services in the church in which novices of the Order took the veil.

On Saturday, January 23, the *Bristol Mercury* carried an account of one of the ceremonies, their reporter, doubtless aware of beliefs among the prejudiced that Catholic females were often immured in religious houses against their will, seeking to add mystery by observing that of the four young ladies "about to bid adieu to the world" one was "said to be possessed of a handsome fortune", and another "was young and beautiful".

On Tuesday last, four young ladies from the North of England, one of whom, a Miss Lynch of Liverpool, is said to be possessed of a handsome fortune, took the white or novice's veil of the Sisters of Penance of the Third Order of St. Dominic, an Establishment of which Order has recently been commenced in this City.

The ceremony was celebrated with much pomp at St. Mary's Roman Catholic Church which was densely crowded with a congregation comprising a great number of Protestants. The altar was gaily decked with flowers and surmounted by an unusual number of tapers. The celebrant, Bishop Right Reverend Doctor Ullathorne, wore his richest sacerdotal vestments, his jewelled mitre, &c. His Lordship was accompanied by two assistant priests from Prior Park, and by the Rev. J. Bonomi, who conducted the ceremonies, Rev. P. O'Farrell leading the choir.

The four ladies, one of whom was young and beautiful, were introduced by some Sisters of the Order, and, having asked of the Bishop in the usual way the habit of religion, His Lordship addressed them on the vocation they were about to enter ... They were about to bid adieu to the world and to devote their lives to the worship of Christ. The Habits of the Order were then fumigated [sic] with incense, sprinkled with Holy Water, and presented by the Bishop to the postulants who retired to throw off the rich lace dresses in which they had been attired and to assume those for their year of probation.

On their return, the novices were accompanied by a procession of about twenty young ladies, clothed in white, crowned with garlands, and each bearing a lighted taper, who officiated as bridesmaids. The white veils were then placed on their heads by the Bishop and Superior of the convent, and, each having been crowned with a wreath of flowers, they retired, carrying tapers, and knelt at the foot of the altar. The 'Veni Creator' was then chanted and the

novices retired in procession as before, which closed the
ceremony.

Three months later the *Bristol Mercury* reported in detail a
similar splendid ceremony conducted by Bishop Ullathorne at St
Mary's when "a young lady took the black veil of the Order of
the Sisters of Penance ... The ceremony was witnessed by a very
crowded congregation, comprising many of the most respected
Protestant females ... the Reverend P. O'Farrell led the choir ..."

The financial difficulties that St Mary's was experiencing in
the early years of its existence led to a rather curious episode that
shed some light on the kinds of services taken on Sundays by Fr
O'Farrell and Fr Cullinan – at least according to one disaffected
parishioner. In 1848 he had taken to absenting himself from St
Mary's, his parish church, and attending Mass, sometimes with
Protestant friends, at St Joseph's which the Jesuits were once
again serving. He set out his reasons in a letter[1] to Bishop
Ullathorne and also offered a remedy for St Mary's problems:

> My Lord, ... I was a member of that congregation some
> time ago, but was obliged to leave that church and go to
> another on account of the length of the sermon. It was often
> half past one to quarter to two before the service was over,
> and this time I could not spare as I am obliged to be home
> at one o'clock.
>
> Mr O' Farrell could preach a very good sermon when he
> chooses ... but now he seldom honours his people with a
> good sermon. They are evidently extempore, and to make
> up for the bad quality he gives a greater quantity. But if I
> say this of Mr O'Farrell what can I say of Mr Cullinan? It
> is certainly out of the frying pan into the fire. Last Sunday I
> heard him preach a sermon one hour and twenty minutes
> long! And what about? Nothing, really nothing. When the
> sermon was over I was so tired and wearied that I could not
> join so fervently in the Mass as I wish to.
>
> Now when one can hear such good and short sermons in
> Trenchard Street is there any inducement to go to St Mary's
> to hear a bad and long one ? ... And if Messrs O'Farrell
> and Cullinan would treat their congregation as if they were

persons of education by writing their sermons beforehand –
by leaving out all hits against the Protestants, at least in the
sermon at Mass ... and instead give us a short, concise and
well written sermon on our Christian duties as men to one
another and as all to God, I am certain ... that the funds of
St Mary's would increase vastly. I and my family would
rejoin it tomorrow, as it is our Parish Church, if we were
assured of hearing a sermon that persons of sense and
education could listen to.

(Signed) 'A Catholic'

I am certain, my Lord, that what I have written is the
sentiments of many of the Catholics of Bristol.

What the outcome of this *cri de coeur* was, alas, we do not
know. In the days before compulsory elementary schooling it
must often have been difficult for a speaker to judge the right
level at which to address his audience, or for how long to pursue
his argument. Certainly the Victorians, who regarded sermons as
a form of entertainment, found long addresses more acceptable
than people would today. The Fathers at St Joseph's seem to have
got it right, if we are to believe the letter writer; certainly his
non-Catholic friends found them more diplomatic!

NOTES

1. Anonymous letter dated October 3, 1848. *Letters & Papers
1837-49*, Clifton Diocesan Archives, 35721, Bristol Record
Office.
   A time of change-over: Dr Hendren was consecrated Vicar
Apostolic of the Western District at St Mary's on September 10,
1848, on the appointment of Dr Ullathorne to the Central District.

Fr Patrick O'Farrell O.S.F., who bought St Mary's for the diocese. This picture has been published elsewhere as a portrait of Fr O'Farrell's colleague, Fr Francis Edgeworth, but the original in the archives is endorsed on the back: "The Rev. P. O'Farrell – For many years one of the Catholic Priests at Bristol & a dear friend & pastor to me. [Signed] J. Dunphy, Febry, 1900." (Bristol Record Office)

CHAPTER 5

The Jesuits Return to Bristol

The last Jesuit to serve at St Joseph's had been William Rowe. He had been in the city two years when, on 16 December, 1830, the Vicar Apostolic, Dr Baines, complained to the Provincial of the Society of Jesus that Fr Rowe had been disrespectful to him as his bishop and had involved himself in a dispute between the Bishop and the Benedictines at Bath; he accordingly asked that he be removed from Bristol. The Provincial, accepting the Bishop's right to have Fr Rowe replaced if he thought him unsuitable, instructed him to leave the city, but found himself unable to send another Jesuit Father to Bristol within the time Dr Baines specified. One thousand four hundred Catholics in the city petitioned on Rowe's behalf. The Provincial, on considering the matter further, felt that Fr Rowe had meant no disrepect to the Bishop, and protested when Dr Baines appointed a non-Jesuit to his post. The dispute went to Rome and dragged on.

While it was recognised that the Bishop's authority must be upheld, there was unease that the Jesuits should be excluded from the mission they had founded in Bristol almost a century earlier, and from the chapel and premises in Trenchard Street which had been paid for largely by the Society's money and the contributions of individual Jesuit priests.

There were some who felt unable to remain silent on this point and Fr O'Farrell (who had been appointed in Fr Rowe's place) became the target of their complaints; it was as though they saw those who came after the Jesuits as usurpers. John Smith, a Catholic residing at 60 College Street, Bristol, a former master at the school, who described himself as Fr Plowden's agent, wrote of "the blundering Pastorals of Bishop Collingridge" and his "tyrannical conduct" in having Fr Plowden removed from St Joseph's; and, as though this had been compounded by Fr Rowe's departure, reminded Bishop Baines of Bishop Walmsley's undertaking in 1789: "We, Charles Walmsley, Bishop of Rama,

V.A., and William Sharrock, Bishop of Telmissium, Coadjutor ... have engaged for ourselves and successors, as far as in our power extend, to admit a member of the house of Liège [Society of Jesus] as an Incumbent of the said Chapel [St Joseph's], as often as the place shall become vacant."[1]

Smith then wrote to the *Bristol Times* on February 6, 1843, the year of St Mary's opening: "I will not be any longer a silent spectator of a monument erected in this my native city, that perpetuates injustice and ingratitude towards a learned and virtuous body of men [the Society of Jesus] against whom not even calumny itself has whispered one error or one fault."

A month after the opening of St Mary's, another Catholic, Joseph Johnson, wrote to Fr O'Farrell accusing him of: altering St Joseph's Chapel; charging for admission to St Mary's; taking the management of the school from the committee and placing it in the hands of one man [Fr Edgeworth], to the disadvantage of the school; and removing the master of the school and depriving him of the secretaryship of the Hibernian Society, of which he had been the founder.

Both Smith and Johnson went so far as to state their case in print, John Smith producing in 1845 a booklet of some 73 pages, in which he was careful to say, however, that whatever it contained was "without the slightest hint from, and without the knowledge of, any member of the Society of Jesus."[2]

Fr O'Farrell, for his part, countered from the pulpit, accusing them and their supporters of meddling, and urging his congregation to have nothing to do with them.

On the death of Dr Baines and the appointment of his successor, Dr Baggs, in January, 1844 it was possible – and clearly desirable – to look at the problem afresh. The new bishop, anxious at Rome's prompting to resolve quickly disputes that caused such tensions (for they were in no sense creative) held discussions with the Provincial and agreed that the Jesuits should return to Bristol at the earliest suitable opportunity. Although Bishop Baggs died the following year, still only 39, his successor, Dr Ullathorne, was equally desirous that the Society should return and he renewed the discussions with the Provincial, Fr Randal Lythgoe. On October 10, 1847 he was able to report:

I have now succeeded in arranging the affairs of the Bristol Mission sufficiently to enable me to invite you to present two missioners for the Trenchard Street Chapel. St Mary's will be continued and another mission will, I trust, be soon established in the direction of Old Market Street.[3]

Since the return of the Jesuits was imminent, Fr O'Farrell set up his presbytery at No.5 Queen's Parade, a road at the foot of Brandon Hill, and Edward Cullinan went to live at No.11 Redcliffe Parade West, which he had previously rented for use as a Mass centre in the early days of the Bedminster mission. He eventually went to America.

At the end of October, 1847, Fr George Bampton S.J. and Fr Thomas Speakman S.J. arrived at Trenchard Street, so restoring the Society's presence in Bristol after an absence of 17 years. George Bampton had qualified as a surgeon and had practised at Plymouth before converting to the Catholic faith and joining the Society of Jesus. He was an able preacher and the author of a book of Lenten discourses, and his growing reputation resulted in his being called to London on December 6, 1849, after only two years in Bristol, to serve at the Jesuits' newly opened church in Farm Street, Mayfair.

Not long after the Jesuits resumed in Bristol, Dr Ullathorne was transferred to Birmingham, to the Central District (as the former Midland District came to be called), and on September 10, 1848 Dr Hendren, the Bishop's Vicar-General and for many years the missioner at Taunton, was consecrated at St Mary-on-the-Quay as Vicar Apostolic of the Western District, in the kind of ceremony that *Felix Farley's Bristol Journal* described as "the most gorgeous of the R.C. Church". A week later the *Bristol Mercury* was reporting the occasion:

The church was crowded by a highly numerous and attentive congregation, comprising many of the principal Protestant families in the neighbourhood. The solemn ceremony occupied from eleven to three o'clock, and was conducted according to the ancient usages of the Catholic Church.

Dr Ullathorne officiated as the consecrating bishop and was assisted by three other bishops. Fr O'Farrell, with two others, was the assistant priest, and about 30 priests from different parts of the diocese were present. The sermon, "My Kingdom is not of this world", was preached by the urbane Dr Wiseman, who two years later became the first Archbishop of Westminster when the hierarchy was at last restored. The musical part of the service comprised a hymn, the Litany of the Saints, and a solemn Te Deum. Bishop Hendren thus became the first Catholic bishop to be consecrated in Bristol for three centuries, and not unnaturally, on the restoration of the hierarchy in 1850, the first bishop of the new diocese of Clifton.

On the death of Bishop Burgess in 1854, Archbishop Errington was appointed Apostolic Administrator of the diocese as an interim measure, and in 1856 he made the following observations about St Mary's in a small 'Journal & Ledger' that he kept: "Debt about £4,000 ... Congregation between 1,500 & 2,000 ... They attend very badly, principally because door money is taken while it is not so in other churches here. The Rector is going to change this custom and have an offertory instead."

In 1852, 134 candidates were Confirmed at St Mary's, and a further 137 in December of 1853. In June of 1857 there were 88 Confirmations, mostly of young people, though the age range spanned 10-60 years. But that year was marked by another significant event: by October the then Bishop of Clifton, Bishop Clifford, thinking Fr O'Farrell's health no longer equal to the demands of the mission at St Mary's, was considering moving him to a less onerous post, and before the year was out Fr O'Farrell had retired to become chaplain to the nuns of St Catherine's Convent, Clifton. Many years later, in the early part of the next century, a parishioner recalled him with affection:

> The Rev. Patrick O'Farrell was pastor at St Mary's when I was baptized in 1848. He was a good pastor and much respected by Protestants as well as Catholics. He loved children and had a fear of scandalizing them. Being of a quick temper he often spoke hastily to those who served his Mass; but one of them told me he would say afterwards: "It was wrong of me to have spoken like that."

He had many cares, for there was a heavy debt on the church; and if £5,000 was raised to buy it from the Irvingites, it must have been borrowed for we were always collecting to pay the interest. I think it was in 1856 that Father OFarrell went abroad [to Rome] to collect money to pay off the debt ... On the following Sunday, at the first Mass, he announced that he would preach two farewell sermons that day, and during the week would be pleased to see anyone who might wish to speak to him.

I shall never forget the sermons and the effect they caused. Some wept, some fainted and were carried out. I shall never forget the heavenly look that came over his beautiful face as he said to me when I paid my visit, "O my child! when you are my age you will know there is nothing worth living for but God alone."[4]

NOTES

1. *Jesuitism & Friarism in Bristol* by John Smith, 1845, *Bristol Papers*, 22/1/3/4, Jesuit Archives, London.
2. Smith, *op. cit.* He was living at the time at Catherine Place, Stokes Croft, Bristol.
3. *Letters & Notices*, Vol.27, Jesuit Archives, London. St Nicholas's, in Lawford's Gate, was opened in 1848.
4. *The Messenger*, June 1903, *Bristol Papers*, 22/1/3/4, Jesuit Archives, London. This was a diocesan publication which carried a supplement of parish news.

The Old Convent in Dighton Street. The Convent of the Sisters of Mercy was closed in 1967. The Sisters have been prominent in the life of St Mary's since 1846. See Chapter 14. (Photo: Sisters of Mercy)

CHAPTER 6

The Society of Jesus Buys St Mary's

In the 1850s the St Mary's mission covered the area from the top of Park Street to Keynsham, and was bounded on one side by St Joseph's and on the other by St Nicholas's, boundaries that were fixed, the parish priest thought, by Bishop Baggs. The surprising reference to Keynsham, situated outside Bristol and some miles from the centre of the city, is explained by the requirement for the St Mary's priest to minister to Catholics at the Poor House in the village. For the most part, the St Mary's congregation lived in the Pithay and the courts and alleys radiating from such streets as Marsh Street, the Quay, Broadmead, and Temple Street.

The average number of boys attending St Mary's School was about 83, and the number of girls from St Mary's who attended school at the convent in Clifton averaged about 40; most were between six and 12 years of age. The parish priest did not think many more could be expected to attend, "considering the extreme poverty of the parents and the early age at which children can add to the common stock."

In 1858 the only priest at St Mary's, Dr English, estimated the number of Catholics in his parish at about 1,500, and the number of Easter communicants at 250-300. Baptisms averaged 75 a year. He considered the proportion of converts as "not great", mentioning five in the previous year.

Every morning the church was open for 9 o'clock Low Mass. On Sundays there was Low Mass at 8.30 a.m., Sung Mass with sermon at 11 a.m., Catechism in the afternoon, and Vespers, Sermon and Benediction in the evening at 6.30.

Part of Dr English's duties was to attend the gaol in the New Cut, and St Peter's Hospital (Poor House) as well as the one at Keynsham. There were four Catholics at St Peter's and he had no difficulty in visiting them, but confessed he had not yet succeeded in obtaining permission to visit anyone in the "Mad Compartment".

In the Diocesan Archives there is an inventory of the church taken in December 1858, and from it we are able to build on the description we were given of the interior of St Mary's at the time of its opening. Fr O'Farrell had retired in 1857, and the beginning of a new era would have provided an opportune moment for a new incumbent to take stock.[1] There would scarcely have been time for many changes of significance to be made, so we may suppose that what we can construct from the items listed will speak of St Mary's as it was during the first 15 years of its life.

The predominant colour was red. At the windows round the body of the church hung red curtains (there were 19 in stock), and amongst the seating were 12 sets of red cushions. The visitor looking at the sanctuary would see the altar against a background of red cloth curtains, suspended from a cornice, and on the floor was a red carpet, although the covering for the altar steps was green.

In the Lady Chapel (or the "Lady Transept" as the inventory styled it), the colour scheme was, not unexpectedly, blue: there were blue stuff curtains, and "best" blue carpet covered the whole area.

Those were the years before the Fathers of the Society of Jesus served the church (although in 1847 they had returned to St Joseph's), and the statues of the great Jesuit saints were not then to be seen. In the sanctuary was a statue of St Peter and one of St Paul (which were later placed at the entrance to the church, in the portico), while over the altar stood a small figure of the Blessed Virgin.

Two large statues of her were to be found elsewhere – one in the Lady Chapel, of course, where there was also a statue of St Joseph, and another across the way in what is known today as the Sacred Heart Chapel but which then was simply referred to as the "Left Transept". A curtain surrounded the foot of this statue.

The left transept was the area used for baptisms. It contained the baptismal font (Bishop Clifford decreed that a picture of St John the Baptist be placed near it) and, surmounted by a small statue of the Blessed Virgin, a tabernacle, which was used as a repository for the holy oils. There was a reminder, too, of the earlier presence (albeit for a few brief years) of another congregation – the old Irvingite font and stand were still in position. In addition to the large statue of Mary there was one of St John. Also sited in this transept was one of the two confessionals in the church, with seating outside for five people.

Strangely, until the time of the 1858 inventory, there is no mention in the archives of the large gallery which runs across the back of the church at the portico end, and which we know did not exist at the time of the dedication of St Mary's. One page of the 13-page inventory is, however, headed "Gallery", and it lists the following furnishings: "organ, 4 benches, 3 chairs, cupboard for music, 10 silk curtains, 2 stuff curtains, 1 music stand, 2 camp stools, 7 kneeling cushions, looking glass, 2 moreen curtains, clock, 10 seats with backs, 10 kneeling forms." All of this, of course, suggests an organ loft; a new organ loft in the left transept was built some 50 years later.

The church had seats for 600 and standing room for 54 more. We learn from the inventory that there were "40 seats with backs, 40 kneeling forms, and 10 forms", and there is mention of another "12 seats and kneeling forms". The cushioned seats were reserved and cost £2.10p per annum to rent; the seats immediately behind these, and the side-seats at the front, cost £1.05p while the charge for centre seats further back was 75p, with special rates for familes. On Sunday mornings the fixed charge at the door was 5p for reserved seats, 3p for the next best, and so on. The annual income of St Mary's was around £220.

Four holy water fonts stood by the doors and there were two poor boxes. A confessional is listed, but its position not indicated. Around the walls were the 14 Stations of the Cross, which had been erected only a year previously. And it was good to see there were still door mats and 12 sets of red cushions: three years earlier the *Bristol Mercury* had, in successive weeks, reported thefts of cushions and a doormat from the church!

There was about the church a signal mark of Victorian furnishing – a wealth of drapery. As we have seen, there were curtains in the nave, and also in the sanctuary and transepts; and on Sundays when the gallery containing the organ had its working complement of organist, organ-blower and choir, all could be unobtrusively housed if need be within a screen of silk curtains.

In other ways, too, the sanctuary was different then. The compiler of the 1858 list refers to a crucifix and canopy over the High Altar (which was of wood) and "4 altar rails", and an altar of oak used as a credence table. There was a brass sanctuary bell and there were three oil paintings, about which no further details are given.

At the front of the sanctuary was an oak preaching stand. Did this suffice? We recall the plaintive letter written to the Bishop ten years earlier by a worshipper exhausted by the prodigious length of Fr O'Farrell's and Fr Cullinan's sermons. Where, then, was the platform worthy of those momentous occasions? If the visitor had descended to the vaults beneath the church he would have found a quantity of lumber and wooden rails, and as he picked his way amongst the paraphernalia and dusty bric-a-brac, he would have come upon, with some surprise, a grander object, discarded but still upright in its dignity – an "oak pulpit, stand and steps", awaiting better days.

By modern standards the schoolroom seems puzzlingly inadequate, reflecting the humble state of elementary education at the time. It had a master's desk and an oak table with drawers, and there was a mahogany writing desk, but apart from a box for ink-stands there was little other sign of scholastic life – save that around the walls were 60 cap pegs. Clearly classroom and cloakroom were one.

Among the enduring characters of Dickens's *Oliver Twist* is Mr Bumble, the parish beadle. St Mary-on-the-Quay had its beadle too. We are not told what his particular responsibilties were, but the duties of a church beadle were, in general, to keep order in the church and to execute the orders of the vestry. We are told that the beadle's coat was kept in the lower vestry. Unfortunately there is no description of it, but the fictional Mr Bumble (drawn from real life we may be sure) can help us here. We know that his coat was wide-skirted, with large brass buttons; it had gold-laced cuffs and gilt-edged lapels. It was important that the coat should help the wearer look authoritative – to reflect "the height and pomp of beadleship." The beadle at St Mary's, like the sacristan, received a quarterly payment.

Outside in the yard, opposite the vestry door, was a piscina and water pump, but the most interesting feature was a cottage,[2] equipped with the modern conveniences of its day – gas fittings and soft-water pump. Although small and narrow, it was the home of the woman who took care of the church and was made available to her as part-payment for her services. It continued to be lived in until 1900 when, by then in a dilapidated state, it was demolished.

Against certain items in the list appear, by way of counter-check, the initials "F.E.". These refer to Dr Ferdinand English, who had been the incumbent at St Mary's since 1857 and was one of the last secular priests to serve there. He was the brother of the coroner for Bath, a city in which his father had been a solicitor. He was educated in the city at Prior Park and at Rome, and was ordained in the year that St Mary's opened. Dr English was remembered by one parishioner as "a bright, cheery little man" who, at the first tea-party held in St Mary's School after he came, said: "I hope you will enjoy yourselves, and if standing on my head will amuse you, I will do it."

A Young Men's Society was started with his encouragement, and he arranged with Bishop Clifford for them to have a room[3] built for their use at the back of the church; the Bishop contributed to the furnishing with the loan of a large bookcase and 247 books from Clifton School. A room for an infants' school was also built at the rear.

Dr English left St Mary's towards the end of 1860 on his appointment as Archbishop of Trinidad[4] – a posting he accepted through a sense of duty – and after his consecration at the cathedral in Clifton sailed for Port of Spain. Sadly, he died in Trinidad two years later at the early age of 43.

There were now in the city centre two Catholic churches,[5] with their own priests and congregations, in close proximity: indeed from the rear of St Mary's to the entrance of St Joseph's there was scarcely 200 yards' distance. Why was this unusual situation, which had existed since 1843, allowed to continue?

We have seen how in 1847, with Fr O'Farrell in agreement, Bishop Ullathorne attempted to sell St Mary's to the Jesuits and turn St Joseph's into schools – a scheme in which the Provincial found serious drawbacks and lost interest. Then early in January

1852 the new Provincial, Fr John Etheridge, on a visit to Trenchard Street learned to his chagrin that St Mary's priests were entertaining the idea of building a school of their own near the church. "[This] will very materially affect the Trenchard Street School," he protested in a letter to Bishop Burgess. "No one who considers the good of religion in Bristol ceases to deplore the nearness of St Mary's Church to St Joseph's."

Could the problem be approached in a different way, and St Mary's closed instead? So fine a building and so recently opened? Not inconceivable, as we shall see later.

With the retirement of Fr O'Farrell, the first rector of St Mary's, and with the departure for Trinidad three years later of his successor, Dr English, Bishop Clifford found room to manoeuvre and he determined to rationalise the situation. On December 1, 1860, three letters on the subject were despatched from Bishop's House.

William Johnson, the Superior at St Mary's, was informed that the distinction between the missions of St Joseph and St Mary was annulled and in future there would be but one mission in the central district, that of St Mary-on-the-Quay under the care of the Fathers of the Society of Jesus. "All parochial rites and services [are] to be performed in the Church of St Mary's on the Quay and not elsewhere." Notice of this change, the Bishop said, was to be given to the congregations of St Mary's and St Joseph's at each service on the first Sunday of Advent.

That same day, a letter to similar effect was sent to the Jesuit Provincial, Thomas Seed, adding that the church of St Joseph would be open only for such additional services "as the necessities of the people might require ... It would be necessary for three efficient priests at least to be employed on this mission. I should consider the proposed arrangement permanent." The Bishop also took the opportunity to inform him that the debt on St Mary's stood at that time at about £1,100.

More precise instructions were given to Fr Johnson in a second letter sent to him the same day: parochial rites were not to be administered at St Joseph's except baptism in cases of emergency; confessions were to be heard at St Mary's, but might be heard also at St Joseph's if necessary.

There were to be special arrangements for the children: there was to be low Mass for them (and others who wished to attend) on Sundays at St Joseph's at 10 o'clock. In the afternoon there was to be Catechism followed by Benediction.

The union of the two missions was to take place at once, "but you need not carry out these injunctions in full till January 1861 so as to give time to settle all questions about choir, seat rents, school communications etc."

These instructions were put into effect, and in 1863 the Provincial felt able to make changes of his own. He informed the Bishop that, should he consent, he intended that Fr Johnson and Fr Matthew McCann of Exeter should change places. During the 14 years he had been in Bristol, Fr Johnson had been assisted by some distinguished Jesuits, among them John Larkin, a great preacher, and John Etheridge, who became Provincial of the Society in the year he left Bristol.

The new Superior at St Mary's, Fr McCann, was an able mathematician and founded the Mathematics Prize at Stonyhurst College.

Normal parish business continued. At this time, 1863, week-day services and a Wednesday evening sermon were instituted at St Mary's. There was much good work going on: an Altar Society was formed; a Men's Guild founded; night schools for boys and young men were started under the management of the Brothers of St Vincent de Paul, and also for women and girls at Dighton Street Convent. A regular succession of Retreats and Tridua were given to members of confraternities and sodalities as well as to the convents at Dighton Street and Arno's Vale and other communities. A useful, if rather specialised, service was provided by Frs Walsh and O'Malley who, apparently, were able to guide many a wayward person along sounder paths by preaching to them in their native tongue, Irish!

The finances of the church were, as usual, under constant review. At the end of 1863, changes were made in the seat-rents: the first three benches were to be 25p a quarter, and the next nine and the front of the gallery 18p. The remaining seats in the body of the church and the gallery were to be 13p a quarter.

St Joseph's now ceased to be used as a public church, and served as a domestic chapel for the Fathers.

One of the Fathers at St Mary's, Antonio Caradonna, was to

be connected with Bristol for many years. He was a Sicilian by
birth, but quickly adapted himself to English life and brought
genial and pleasant ways to his work, especially with the young.
Zealous and kind of heart, he found a sympathetic response
amongst the boys, whom he gathered together into a guild, and
who affectionately changed his name to "Caledonia".

One hundred and fifty-one candidates were confirmed by
Bishop Clifford on December 4, 1864, and we know that as the
season of Easter approached each year it was the custom for Fr
McCann to choose, at the Bishop's request, three poor boys from
the district of St Mary's and three from that of St Joseph's and
instruct them to report to Bishop's House at the appointed time
with a certificate testifying to good conduct and diligent
attendance at school, to be measured for the "usual gift of clothes
etc. from the Bishop" to be given on Maundy Thursday at the
Cathedral.

Such gifts were not, as is clear, commemorative alone, but
practical assistance to decent families struggling in hardship.
Many of Bristol's Catholics were amongst the poorest of the
city's poor.[6] At the time of the opening of St Mary's, many parts
of the city, including Clifton, were totally without sewerage, and
where there was drainage it led directly into the harbour and the
Frome. The death rate in Bristol of 31 per 1,000 of the population
was exceeded only by Liverpool and Manchester. The hovels of
the poor to whom the Jesuit, Robert Plowden, had brought
comfort at the turn of the century were renewed in the
overcrowded tenements of succeeding years – perhaps 10 families
in a house, one to each room. Amongst the alleys in St James's
Back, where in the previous century Father Scudamore had set up
the first Catholic chapel, 16 people were found by the sanitary
officers to be living in one small room; elsewhere in a court as
many as 50 or 60 persons had the use of just one closet. In 1866
29 people in the city died of cholera. Until regulations, stemming
from the Public Health Act, put a stop to it, children as young as
five and six years of age had been selling articles in the streets
until 10 and 11 o'clock at night, often in the winter. And
sometimes the School Board Officer had to intervene to
remonstrate with parents who beat their children with a strap for
failing to earn enough money on the streets. Barefooted poverty

haunted the young lives of many.

On July 16, 1865, Fr Dykes (Fr McCann's successor) announced that in future there would be an offertory at all services at St Mary's to defray the expenses of the mission. There was also another development in the story of seat-rents: on August 13 it was stated that in future there would be free admittance to the benches on the sides but not in the centre of the church.[7]

Shortly after this, two particularly significant events occurred. In 1869 the First Vatican Council was held, and the doctrine of papal infallibility soon emerged as the most important subject of discussion. It had been part of Catholic awareness for centuries, but now received formal expression in the Council's Decree on Infallibility in 1870. In Bristol most of the clergy accepted the dogma without difficulty, but Bishop Clifford's attitude throughout the debate resulted in many Catholics in the city feeling confused; it seemed that their bishop was not comfortable with the new decree (as indeed he was not) and they sought guidance. Clifford, along with Archbishop Errington, never formally declared against the doctrine but duly acknowledged the infallibility of the Pope to be part of the official teaching of the Catholic Church.[8]

Over 20 years earlier, overtures had been made to the Jesuits to take over St Mary-On-the-Quay; by 1869, the initiative was coming from the Jesuits themselves with an offer to buy the church for £2,500 provided, once again, the vendors could show good title, free from incumbrances. The reply was somewhat unexpected. A letter from Bishop Clifford to the Provincial, Alfred Weld, carried a rebuff – a decision not to sell "on the terms proposed." He had other plans. "It now seems certain that ultimately St Joseph's will be a much better site for Church and house than St Mary's." At the opportune moment St Mary's would be sold at its market price and the mission established elsewhere in the city. And, as if to reinforce his message that St Mary-on-the-Quay had no long-term future as a Catholic church, he added: "Even if the Society should at any time retire from serving St Mary's I do not contemplate opening a secular mission again in that part of the town."

Such was to be the new strategy. But almost two years later

the players were rehearsing the scene yet again, and this time all agreed that with a little rewriting it would do. A Memorandum for the sale of St Mary's to the Society of Jesus was signed on May 29, 1871. Fifteen hundred pounds was to be paid at once and £1,200 left upon the property by way of a loan at four per cent. The signatories were Bishop Clifford, Thomas Dykes, the Superior at St Mary's, and Henry Foley, the great Jesuit archivist at Farm Street, signing from the Society's address in London. By August 3, 1871 the purchase was complete, and the Jesuits once again had their own church in Bristol.

At this time (Queen Victoria had now reigned for 35 years) Irish immigrants in Bristol, as in other cities, could often only obtain forms of employment involving hard manual work and perhaps irregular hours. But they were determined to observe the old customs and attend Sunday Mass if at all possible. Those engaged on the Saturday night shift at the gasworks at Canon's Marsh, which ended at 6 o'clock on Sunday morning, were not to be denied: the children took their fathers' best suits to the gasworks and the men cleaned themselves, changed their clothes and marched along the quayside to the special early Sunday morning Mass at St Mary's.

People took their entertainment by way of school and sodality tea-parties, simple plays and well-organised concerts. In 1873 a lending library was opened in the St Mary's schoolroom and the following year mothers' meetings were inaugurated.

The Fathers were regarded as learned men, some thought of as personalities. Fr Thomas Meyrick, who left Bristol after three years in residence, was a convert and a man of scholarly attainments, and one of St Mary's parishioners remembered walking with him later when the good Father was over 80 years of age. It was a walk of some 10 miles and the old gentleman enlivened the journey with numerous anecdotes, quotations from the Greek and Latin classics, and snatches of old, favourite songs.

A much-needed addition was made to the presbytery, and during the building operations the priests lived at Springfield House in Cotham, which had been bequeathed to Fr Dykes in 1872, for the use of the mission, by Mr John Fergus Green, a member of the St Mary's congregation. It was a fine dwelling in Cotham Road with a portico entrance, five bedrooms, two dressing-rooms and servants' quarters; in the grounds were green-houses, a summer-house, coach-houses and stabling. The property was usually let to tenants on a long lease and proved to be useful as security for raising money for the parish when need arose. It was sold in 1921.

Bishop Clifford officiated at a service in September 1873, when a new statue of the Sacred Heart was placed in the church and the whole parish was consecrated to our Lord under that title.

Fr James Splaine, who was appointed to St Mary's in that year, was accorded a special honour when, in 1876, he was appointed president of the Temperance Society, and to mark the occasion he invited Cardinal Manning to give a lecture at the Colston Hall in aid of its funds and its work, Bishop Clifford being in the chair. Fr Splaine formed a Temperance Confraternity and arranged for it to have a banner of St Patrick made by Roman artists, and 800 silvered medals, with the likeness of Pius IX on one side, sent from Rome. Before dispatch the medals were blessed by the Pope, and Splaine's correspondent at the Collegio Inglese expressed the hope that he could arrange for the banners to be similarly blessed, adding: "Your experiences amongst the drunkards are woeful." A further letter spoke of success:

> I am glad to inform you that yesterday, March 8th, your banner of St Patrick was presented at the Vatican to the Holy Father, and was blessed by His Holiness for your Temperance Confraternity ... As these Roman Artists live from hand to mouth I shall be glad if you can send me at once a cheque for £12 in payment of the Banner ...

The prevalence of drunkenness amongst the poor, who often resorted to it as an escape from the wretchedness of their lives, was one of the great social concerns of the Victorians. They attempted to combat it through the Temperance Society and similar bodies which under various names (e.g. Band of Hope) persisted until well into the twentieth century, often spearheaded by the drive and commitment of religious organisations.

Until this time the choir at St Mary's had received some form of payment, but in 1877 the 'paid choir' sang for the last time and was superseded by a voluntary one.

A year later, there came to Bristol from Farm Street Church a priest whose arrival and work in St Mary's parish was little remarked upon at the time, and whose stay was so short his name did not appear amongst the St Mary's priests listed in the city directory for 1878. Unbeknown to most of the congregation and the country at large he was a poet – and one of much originality. He left Bristol to work in Oxford, and in 1884 was appointed to the chair of Greek at Dublin University. It was not until 30 years after his death that his poems were published and an international reputation established. He was the great Jesuit poet, Gerard Manley Hopkins.

A census taken by the *Western Daily Press* in 1881 revealed the numbers attending worship at the main morning service and evening service in every church in Bristol on Sunday 30, of that year.[9] The numbers in the four Roman Catholic churches then in existence totalled 3,432, made up as follows:

	MORNING	EVENING	TOTAL
Pro-Cathedral	740	682	1,422
St Mary-on-the-Quay	500	522	1,022
St Nicholas	482	217	699
Holy Cross	132	157	289
	1,854	1,578	3,432

The morning figures refer to the 9.30 Mass; there were about 140 at each of the earlier Masses, and 400 at 11 a.m. Catechism in the afternoon was attended by some 200 children.

Many Catholic families in those days lived within walking distance of the church, and the children were able to go to their own Mass at St Mary's on Sundays. They were used to being greeted at the door by someone from the church holding out his hand and saying: "A penny, please!" When his hand was full the collector would empty the contents into his pocket and resume the operation. Paying in this way was not made a condition of entry, but people were expected to contribute. It was an established practice in many churches.

The boys would sit one side and the girls the other, so filling the centre of the church. At the end of the benches were slots into which were inserted banners of the various Guilds – St Patrick, St Mary, St George . . .

A register was kept of children who were late or absent and this would be consulted when the time came to decide which children could attend the Christmas party or go on the outing to Weston.

These final decades of the nineteenth century were a period when plan and counter-plan for the development of the city continually came before the authorities for approval. Would it be possible, for instance, (it would certainly be desirable) to eliminate the zig-zag pattern of roads that ran between the top of Park Street and the Assize Courts in Broad Street, an area that embraced St Mary's, and St Joseph's and its presbytery? For years the Mayor had quietly been buying up property in the area for this purpose: now the planners took a hard look at Trenchard Street. A letter referring to the Catholic property there had already gone to the Diocesan architect, Charles Hanson. He had, it seems, ignored it. Another followed on September 2, 1878: it was the wish of the Mayor to see the streets in that locality improved, the letter explained, and for that purpose he was willing to buy the presbytery and garden in Trenchard Street ("not for private gain"). "He does not wish to buy the chapel." A letter from Hanson to Fr Hill alerted him to the plans, and the St Mary's rector in turn informed the Provincial, Fr Purbrick, in London. The possibilities were considered. "Do you think you could sell the house and retain the Hall, and if so would that be of any advantage and what?" asked Purbrick. And then, concerning the Mayor's offer: "Hold out for the higher terms." So time passed – and nothing changed. But it had been an unsettling and time-consuming episode.[10]

Then, in October 1883, a plan was mooted – the Bristol and South Counties railway scheme – which, if passed, would have meant the end of St Mary-on-the-Quay, for the church would have had to give place to the proposed new Central Railway Station. Although generally welcomed by Bristolians, the plans were abandoned by the Great Western Railway and London &

South Western Railway, who agreed not to oppose each other. Even supposing generous compensation had been granted, no new site for the church would have been better than the existing one in Colston Avenue, notwithstanding its disadvantages.

In 1884 Bishop Clifford issued regulations to the clergy to be observed for the celebration of Midnight Mass at Christmas in churches and chapels in the diocese:

1. It must be a High Mass, or at least a Missa Cantata.
2. Holy Communion must not be administered.
3. Admission must be by tickets carefully distributed.
4. In cases where few Catholics could attend, and where in consequence the attendance would consist mainly of Protestants, the service must not take place.
5. Where the priest deems it necessary the services of a policeman at the door must be secured.
6. Notice of the service will be given with other notices in the church on the previous Sunday, but all advertisements whether in the newspaper or by placards or handbills or in any other way whatsoever are strictly prohibited.

These instructions, designed to ensure that the Midnight Mass was conducted in seemly circumstances, continued to be issued in subsequent years.

During the Universal Jubilee of 1886, proclaimed by Pope Leo XIII "in order that thereby the minds and hearts of men may be reformed ...", the Plenary Indulgence of the Jubilee (as with previous Jubilees) could be gained by Catholics in Bristol observing certain rules on fasting, almsgiving and Confession, and by making six visits to a church in the city: "two visits to the Pro-Cathedral, two to St Mary's on the Quay, and two to St Nicholas, Pennywell Road and there for some space of time to offer devout prayers " – Bishop Clifford ordered the notice to this effect to be read in all churches and to be "affixed to the Church doors."

NOTES

1. "When, in 1858, the Franciscans were succeeded by secular priests at Trenchard Street, a number of papers and manuscripts were about to be removed, and during the examination of these a perfect copy of the Hereford Missal was found, the only edition known to be in existence. Its rareness and value were sufficiently tested by the fact that its sale realised £300, and that it was purchased by the British Museum." *Letters & Notices*, Vol.27, p.182. Jesuit Archives, London. The sale of this missal (now in the Bodleian Library, Oxford) was the occasion of a bitter dispute between Bishop Clifford and Bishop Brown of Newport & Menevia. See Chapter 4 of *Bishop Clifford* by J.A. Harding, 1991, Clifton Diocesan Archives.
2. "The site on which it stood was probably at first open and airy; for years however it had been shut in behind a lofty wall, which deprived it of air, view, or light." The caretakers who lived there were a person called Tyne, who was succeeded by Stephen Griffin and his wife, and then by Mr & Mrs Santary, who lived there for a considerable time and brought up a family there. It was condemned by the sanitary authority as unfit to be inhabited and closed in 1889. Fr Brown then ordered it to be pulled down as endangering the lives of the school children who played in the yard. *Letters & Notices*, Vol.27, pp.181-182, Jesuit Archives, London.
3. "I propose to grant them a lease of the premises for 1/- per an. for 7 years, on condition of their laying out £70 on the premises." *Bishop Clifford, letter to Dr English, July 14, 1858*. Clifton Diocesan Archives.
4. In 1860 Archbishop Errington, in dispute with Cardinal Wiseman, was dismissed as his coadjutor and offered the Archbishopric of Trinidad, which he declined.
   There is a portrait of Archbishop English in the library at the Bishop's residence, St Ambrose, in Bristol.
5. "Now ... we possess the commanding church of St Mary's-on-the-Quay, the fruit of the energetic zeal of F.O'Ferrall [sic], who deserves much better support. We retain the original church of St Joseph, that joyful mother of children, and having 2,000 communicants attached." George Oliver, *op. cit.*

6. "The numbers and destitution of the Catholic poor in Bristol, probably exceed, comparatively, those of any large town in England." Annual Report of Bristol and Clifton Catholic Poor Schools, 1850. *Letters & Papers 1850-1859*, Clifton Diocesan Archives, Bristol Record Office.

7. *Bristol Papers*, 20/5/4/2, Jesuit Archives, London.

8. "At the First Vatican Council he spoke to great effect, particularly on the issue of Papal Infallibility. This he saw as disturbing the proper balance between the Pope and the college of bishops, and as antagonising unnecessarily those Protestants who were well disposed to the Church. He nevertheless remained loyal and this gave him an added influence in the post-conciliar Church." J.A. Harding, *op. cit.* (Abstract). Clifton Diocesan Archives.

Mgr. John Bonomi V.G. wrote to Bishop Clifford on November 13, 1870 saying: "Everyone [i.e. "The foremost priests in the Diocese"] says that in the confessional and out of it, they are perpetually asked what the Bishop believes."

In the course of his reply on November 17, 1870, Clifford said: "The Pope has published the decree on Infallibility, and I consciously bow to his authority." *Ibid.*, pp.431, 435.

9. The most remarkable figures for the Anglican churches in Bristol were those of St Paul's, Coronation Road, with 1,164 at the morning service and 1,152 attending in the evening. A century later the church is an interesting example of the changes that have taken place in many parishes of the Church of England, St Paul's now being one of three churches in the Bedminster Team Ministry.

10. The letters referred to in this episode are those in the *Bristol Papers*, 20/5/2/2, Jesuit Archives, London.

CHAPTER 7

The Final Decade
of the Nineteenth Century

June 27, 1890 found one of St Mary's priests, Fr Ignatius Grant, preoccupied with putting the final touches to an important speech he was to make that night. The occasion was the celebration to mark the centenary of the opening of St Joseph's, Trenchard Street, at which he was to deliver the main address before a distiguished audience, including the Bishop of Clifton, the Right Reverend Dr Clifford.[1]

The choice of Father Grant was a wise one: he was an excellent speaker, attractive to Catholics and Protestants alike. If it was announced in the local press that he was to preach the following Sunday, the church would be crowded for the occasion, and those unable to get inside the building would stand on the portico and pavement below – and on the other side of the water too! For when the big central doors of the church were open all could hear his voice.

His idiosyncrasies were part of a colourful personality. He enjoyed taking snuff, and if when in church he needed more light by which to read there was a practical solution to hand: he would – anticipated by the thoughts of a knowing congregation – fetch a candle from the altar.

He was, too, an antiquarian. His most interesting work in Bristol was the subject of an article written for the Jesuit magazine, *The Month*, in October 1887. Entitled "From Oxford to Douay", it was concerned in part with St Catherine's Hospital, founded in the hamlet of Bedminster near Bristol about 1220 as a resting place for pilgrims on their way to Glastonbury or to shrines in Bristol itself: "It was sufficiently endowed to afford a dole to everyone on his way – a piece of bread, some good Cheddar cheese, and a good draught of cider." But what was of immediate concern to Fr Grant and other antiquarians in the Bristol of 1887 was that St Catherine's, or what remained of it

FATHER GRANT'S LECTURE ON 1790.

FATHER ROBERT PLOWDEN.

PRICE SIXPENCE.

Robert Plowden's picture on the cover of the printed version of Fr Grant's lecture delivered in 1890. He was a controversial figure, but one of the great names in the history of the Catholic Church in Bristol. (Jesuit Archives) (the chapel had been pulled down in the reign of Elizabeth 1), was about to be demolished and replaced by a huge factory belonging to a firm who were to become amongst the greatest employers in the history of the city. Writing his article from St Mary's presbytery he observed:

> Alas! to-day, whilst I write these words, they are pulling down the remains of the hostelry (Feb. 12, 1887). By Tuesday next not a "wrack" will be left behind. All is absorbed by an immense fabric of Bristol "Bird's Eye" tobacco, and by the great firm of Wills and Company.

The sketches that he and Eric Leslie (another Jesuit priest at St Mary's) made of St Catherine's Hospital are the only pictorial record in existence of the historic place, founded six and a half centuries earlier.

Fr Grant had first come to St Mary's in 1867, but for a year only. Ten years later, at the time of the opening of St Bonaventure's, he rejoined the staff of St Mary's, this time with Fathers Clifford, Sherlock and Hill.

He had prepared his address carefully and was able to tell of the renowned Plowden family and their service to the Church, and particularly that of Robert,[2] St Joseph's first priest; he then sketched the history of Catholicism in Bristol since the Reformation. His remarks on the kinds of services which Catholics used in the 1790s are of particular interest:

> Besides Holy Mass and Sermon, preceded by the usual Prayers before Mass and the oblation, "And now, O God, we prepare to offer Thee," there was generally the Psalter of Jesus and Catechism in the afternoon. Even in London you would hardly have found Vespers. There was no evening service anywhere. There was only a rare Benediction of the Blessed Sacrament. As yet the Rosary was rarely said in public.

1790 also saw the beginning of the general observation of Good Friday in Bristol by shops closing on that day, a practice followed by only a few in the past.

Fr Grant singled out certain of St Mary's priests for special mention and had an interesting note on Fr William Maher:

> 1857. Father William Maher, a native of Bristol, talented and pious son of a talented and pious father, Mr Jeremiah Maher. He was connected with the family of Newtons and Sir Isaac Newton. This excellent religious, beloved by all his brethren, was here but for a very brief year; but even so, illustrated his native town, for he was of great musical and artistic talent. Good preacher and giver of retreats, he was a sound director, with great prudence and discretion. Perhaps no Jesuit in London had greater influence, and few were more esteemed in the Province for his geniality and wit. He died at Paris and is buried in the cemetery of Mont-Parnasse.

An interesting addendum might be given here about Fr Maher's father, Jeremiah.[3] He lived at 25 Dove Street and is the Jeremiah Maher we met earlier who with his two daughters would sing at the services at the young Bedminster mission, then served by St Mary's priests. In the Jesuit Archives in London there is a collection of correspondence presenting Fr Robert Plowden's case in his celebrated dispute with Bishop Collingridge, which, at the Bishop's request, led to Robert's eventual removal by the Jesuits from St Joseph's in 1815. The name on the front cover of the collection is that of the compiler – J. Maher, Bristol. We learn from the contents that he was present in St Joseph's at the Sunday Mass at which Fr Plowden criticised the Bishop's Lenten letter saying, so the Bishop himself later expressed it, that "it was the duty of inferiors to come forward and correct the Bishop." Six years after Robert had been forced to leave the city the young Jeremiah wrote to him, and received a reply thanking him for his friendly letter and again stating his grounds for challenging the Bishop. Robert was then in his eighty-second year and living in comparative obscurity near Coventry. There were many Catholics in the city (and Protestants too) who, like Jeremiah Maher, recalled Fr Plowden with affection and who, soon after his removal from St Joseph's, had pleaded for his return.

When Fr Grant's speech was published in 1890 he saw fit to

print (in parentheses) his audience's reactions to parts of it. Such little asides are not without interest. They reveal, for instance, the natural patriotism of the Catholics of the time, whereas for their own ends and as part of the anti-Catholic tradition that had developed since the Reformation, their opponents often sought to question it, with their talk of the need to defend "civil and religious liberties":[4]

> In this year too [1790], one name had come with effulgence and honour into every English home and to every English fireside ... Horatio Nelson! (great applause).

Speaking of religious tolerance towards Catholics he remarked:

> "Papists found charity amongst us!" And that charity has continued for a century, and does honour to the liberality and spirit of "fair play" shown to the Catholic body by the good and antique city of Bristol (applause).

That he should show his audience's warm appreciation of this "liberality and spirit of 'fair play'" towards them indicates that it was not something that even then, 60 years after the Catholic Relief Act, could be taken for granted. Some still saw Catholicism as a threat. The Bristol Church Association, for instance, with headquarters at the Royal Insurance buildings in Corn Street, was established "to uphold the doctrines, principles, and order of the United Church of England and Ireland; and to counteract the efforts being made ... to assimilate her services to those of the Church of Rome." Another organisation, the Lay Protestant Missionary Association, using its own foot-soldiers, preferred a more direct approach, diffusing "Gospel and Protestant Truth amongst the Roman Catholics and Protestants, by means of house visiting, discussion classes and tract distribution."

But Fr Grant's speech that night was in no way controversial, any more than Fr Plowden's when he spoke hopefully of Catholic and Protestant accord 100 years before. Fr Grant died at St Beuno's College, North Wales, in 1904, in his 85th year.

Jane Maher, Jeremiah's daughter, was in 1892 in her 78th year and living in St Joseph's Convalescent Home in Bournemouth, from where she entered into frequent correspondence with Fr Clifford at St Mary's. She fondly recalls the old days – how her mother was born on the outskirts of Bristol at Hanham, near to where their ancestor Sir Isaac Newton lived, and how she married Jeremiah on February 22, 1813. Jane went to church at St Joseph's with her mother and always occupied the seat Fr Plowden had allocated her, and regularly paid for her sitting. In the early days of St Mary's the family rarely went to church there, although it was nearer their home, doubtless because Jeremiah felt the Jesuits, particularly in the persons of Fr Plowden and after him, Fr Rowe, had been wronged.

At Jane's request Fr Clifford and the family solicitor went to her house in Dove Street to make arrangements for the disposal of her property. To assist them she listed the articles to be found in the rooms and described some of the pictures, which then led her to recall how the famous artist, Francis Danby,[5] used to visit them and was particularly taken with one of the scenes he saw.

She remembered when Fr Cullinan preached his last sermon at St Mary's, in 1850, and how when he left for America he took with him a beautiful stole worked in silk tent stitch by her sister, Agnes. Clearly a labour of love, for they had recorded the number of stitches – 66,760! But Jane had an offering of her own: "The Madonna I worked for St Mary's was in wool," she added shyly. Oh dear! She hoped good Fr Clifford would not think her vain!

As the years passed, the Drawbridge across the harbour in the centre of Bristol was proving more and more inadequate. Narrow and dangerous, busy with the crossings of vehicles and horse-drawn trams, it was failing to cope with the growing demands of the traffic constantly channelled through it; the alternative was to use the Stone Bridge, the other side of St Mary-on-the-Quay. Frequently, indeed, all was brought to a halt, perhaps for 20 minutes or more as the Drawbridge was swivelled to allow the passage of ships. These vessels, brigs and schooners, often unloaded their cargoes in front of St Mary's, the approaches to which were further impeded by the wagons that arrived alongside. Bold measures were needed to resolve the various problems; it was proposed that a stretch of waterway that had, perhaps, outlived its usefulness should be converted to dry land.[6]

In May 1891 Royal Assent was given to a bill enabling the city council to fill in the quay from the Drawbridge to Quay Head, in the direction of Broadmead, by arching over the water space. The work was set in hand and completed at a cost of £15,493, while the old drawbridge was replaced with a permanent bridge costing £8,065. The river Frome flowing just beyond St Mary's steps was, by May 6, 1893, no longer to be seen. The metamorphosis was complete.

So in that anniversary year of St Mary's – 50 years since its dedication – it was possible to look across from the portico of the church and see, directly ahead, not the familiar waterside scene – the bollards dividing road from quayside, the piles of ships' ballast, barges on the water and small-masted ships, and the 'Ethel' moored near the Drawbridge a few feet away – but a new central space later to be set out as a pleasure garden with ornamental seats and bandstand. It was soon called, unofficially, Magpie Park, after the popular weekly, *The Magpie*, whose offices were a few doors away from the church.

But before this further development took place, the newly created ground was occupied for six months of that year by a huge wooden building which, extending some 520 feet in length and 110 feet wide, reached the frontage of St Mary's. It had been erected to house the Bristol Industrial and Fine Arts Exhibition – a grand affair that cost £100,000 and attracted 20,000 visitors a week, over 500,000 people in all.

A large electric clock, an early one, crowned the entrance, and in the principal streets electric arc lamps were beginning to replace the gas lights of old. St Mary's parishioners pondered the advantages of the new electricity. In an advertisement Messrs King, Mendham & Co., Electric Light Engineers, argued powerfully that people should use it in their homes. Did they realise that there "would be no danger of explosions" and the light would be immediately extinguished if their servant accidentally broke a lamp? That their lace and paper shades would never get scorched, and that cook could have a light directly over her saucepan or in her oven? Even if they had a higher electricity bill at the end of the quarter, they would have no paper hanging or whitewashing to do! It was worth considering!

Of the businesses that had flanked St Mary's in 1843, only three now remained: William Wright & Sons, wine merchants, were still next door, and Pickfords a few buildings away; William Hardcastle had gone to his rest, but he had left the Artichoke Tavern in good hands. Even nearer was a newcomer, Rupert House, where an eight-page weekly of gossip and scandal, *The Magpie*, was produced. Other journals, however, were more prominent in 1893: the *Bristol Mercury*, established in 1790 (the year in which St Joseph's was built), was now published daily, price one penny, and claimed to be the most widely read newspaper in Bristol. The *Western Daily Press* made a different but equally large claim: it represented, it said, the commercial life of Bristol and had the largest circulation in the West of England.

Catholics were saddened during the year to learn of the death of Dr. Clifford, Bishop of the diocese for 36 years. He had played a leading part in the First Vatican Council and was arguably the most distinguished of the Bishops of Clifton. He had been a good friend to the Jesuit Fathers, but his successor, Dr. Brownlow, was equally supportive of the Society, and after his consecration a reception was held for him at the presbytery in Trenchard Street.

In 1893 Fr Thomas Greenan became Superior. He had come to Bristol from Edinburgh and through his efforts and those of his colleagues – Fr J. Ross, Fr O'Gorman, and Fr W. Edgcome – he more than doubled the congregation of St Mary-on-the-Quay, a contributory factor no doubt being that the vicinity of the church became a centre for the tramway system, so that for a small fare St Mary's could be reached from any part of the city.[7]

It was felt necessary to respond to this increase in congregation by redecorating the entire church and making it more presentable. How was the money to be raised? Bazaars had great popular appeal in the Victorian age and it was with no little pride that for years afterwards St Mary's people spoke of the splendid bazaar – the "All the Year Round " bazaar, they called it – which was held in the Colston Hall, hired for a week in 1896 from October 20 to 26. Admission was 2.5p all day, half price for children.

The souvenir programme contained 50 pages, with many

advertisements, and listed 31 patrons for the bazaar including the Dowager Duchess of Newcastle, the Marquess of Ripon, the Earl of Denbigh and the Countess of Bantry. The Executive and General Committees comprised 78 names.

The opening ceremony was performed on the Tuesday afternoon at 3 p.m. by Bishop Brownlow and the Provincial of the Society, Fr Francis Scoles, with Fr Greenan as chairman; on the following days there were other dignitaries and chairmen. The band of the 5th Gloucesters played each day and there were stalls, attractions such as the Shooting Jungle, Grand Washing Competition and Hat-Trimming Competition, concerts with orchestral performance and variety programmes. Thursday, for instance, was Comic Concert Night with, amongst others, Miss Eppie Cuthbert, "The youngest pianist out of London. Aged 5 years."[8] At the bottom of each page of the programme of events was some suitable exhortation. Who, for instance, could fail to stiffen the sinews as he read: "St Mary's expects that all this day will do their duty"? From this celebrated event several hundred pounds were raised to fund church projects.

For some time the Society of Jesus had wanted to set up grammar schools in cities where they already had a mission, and Fr Greenan saw the possibility of establishing one in Bristol. At that time, however, Bishop Brownlow was negotiating for the Irish Christian Brothers to take a lease on Prior Park and, fearing that they would look on a Jesuit school in neighbouring Bristol as a rival establishment, he felt unable to support the idea while the negotiations had a chance of success. Eventually the Christian Brothers assumed responsibilty for Prior Park in Bath and also in 1896 opened a school, St Brendan's College, in Bristol.[9]

The number of Catholics living in the district, which was becoming more and more a commercial and business area, gradually diminished as they looked for homes elsewhere, but the congregation, particularly on Sunday evenings, continued to increase, thanks to the good tram service, an effective choir, and "the adoption of a more general system of congregational singing." Through Fr Greenan's efforts the congregation at St Mary's had more than doubled by 1898, when Thomas Brown became the new Superior.

NOTES

1. "William Clifford (Bishop of Clifton 1857-1893) was one of the most influential prelates in the 19th century English Catholic Church. Consecrated at the age of 33, he was the youngest English bishop since the Reformation ... He possessed a fine theological and legal mind, was moderate in his opinions and of an attractive personality." J.A. Harding, *op. cit.,* 1991.

2. Robert Plowden S.J. (1740-1823), devoted to St Joseph's and his flock, was never reluctant to engage in controversy in defence of, as he saw it, the truth. Dr Oliver said: "... it brings tears to the eyes, and agony to the heart, to witness this champion of religion ... forgetting his duty so far as to refuse to publish, on 5th December, 1813, and, again, to denounce the Lenten Pastoral of his bishop, dated Taunton, 1st February, 1815, from the opinion that erroneous doctrine was lurking under those official documents ... Forced to bid farewell where he had laboured so long and so successfully, this lion-hearted but wrong-headed old man took refuge in the Midland District." George Oliver, *op. cit.,* p.383.

William Strickland, Administrator of the ex-Jesuits in Fr Plowden's time, said of him in a letter to J. Couche in December 1799: "... there is perhaps not a better missionary in England." Praise indeed since at the same time Strickland found him a difficult man to deal with and was in serious dispute with him about the Bristol property. See *William Strickland and the Suppressed Jesuits* by Geoffrey Holt S.J., 1988.

3. Bishop Baines had regarded Jeremiah Maher as one of the ringleaders of the Catholic group in the city opposing him in his dispute with the Jesuits over the ownership of the Bristol Mission. In a letter to Rome explaining the causes of the tensions in the local Catholic community at the time, he described Jeremiah as "an under-clerk in a fire-insurance office, also a freemason who has not approached the Sacraments for the last fifteen years." His comments on the other three people he named were that one was "formerly a lay-brother among the Jesuits," another was "by trade a pianoforte tuner and by profession a freemason," and the third was "a man milliner who is supposed to be living with another man's wife." He described the four of them as "turbulent

mischief-makers". Clifton Diocesan Archives.

4. Consider, for instance, the situation in John Scudamore's time when he was the only Catholic priest in the city and Thomas Newton was Bishop of Bristol. Dr Newton was outspoken in his opposition to the Catholic Church and in his dislike of the Jesuits (such as Fr Scudamore) in particular. Addressing his fellow clergy on the subject of "The increase of popery, 1766'" he wrote: "It cannot be presumed or expected that such turbulent spirits [the Jesuits] ... should ever become loyal subjects to those of a different religion." *The Works of the Right Rev. Thomas Newton D.D., Lord Bishop of Bristol & Dean of St Paul's, London*, (Charges), Vol.2, 1782.

5. Francis Danby, who was born in Ireland, first came to Bristol in 1813 when he had yet to establish his reputation as an artist, and was so poor that on arrival he had insufficient money to pay for a night's lodging. In all he exhibited 46 pictures at the Royal Academy. Thackeray and Disraeli praised his work – imaginative, poetic landscapes, including scenes of the neighbourhood of Bristol. He left England for the continent in 1829 and in 1847 settled in Exmouth where he lived until his death. Jane Maher would have been 14 when the artist went abroad.

6. Doubtless parts of the river had become polluted in years past: prisoners in the Bridewell in Fr Scudamore's time would complain in summer of the stench from the open sewer, but the building of the Floating Harbour had solved problems caused by the tides. Just before the outbreak of the Second World War in 1939, more of the river was covered over and used temporarily for car parking; today there are flower beds and an improved road system.

7. As long as Bristol had trams, the centre of the city was always referred to as the 'Tramway Centre'.

8. Among other performers were "the renowned Brothers Josen (Banjo Soloists) and Mr Willie Evans (Negro Comedian, in his famed Bicycle Song)." *Souvenir Programme, Bazaar 1896, Bristol Papers*, 22/1/3/4, Jesuit Archives, London.

9. Fr Greenan had represented to Dr Brownlow that Prior Park and the city of Bristol were different places, and quite sufficiently removed from each other to admit of the existence of a separate and distinct school in both. "The upshot was that the Brothers

took Prior Park and at the same time opened a school in Bristol itself." *Letters and Notices*, Vol.27, p.178, Jesuit Archives, London.

CHAPTER 8

A Victorian Funeral

In the small hours of September 1, 1898, William Scantlebury, respected amongst his peers as the caretaker of Bristol's biggest concert theatre, the Colston Hall, was soundly asleep at his home in Trenchard Street. So too, no doubt, were his neighbours at number 21, the presbytery of St Mary-on-the-Quay. But around the corner at 21 Colston Street, events were unfolding that for many would turn the dark hours of that early morning into a vivid nightmare.

The premises of Robert Clarke & Co., wholesale and export clothiers, were extensive, rising three storeys above the ground floor and stretching from the Colston Hall to Trenchard Street, but the busy commerce anticipated for the day ahead would never now take place. Bales of cloth fed the flames of that night's great fire, which then spread rapidly, bursting into the darkness and searching noisily across the roof tops. It was a quarter past two. The fire brigade reached the scene too late to contain the flames and, the conflagration spreading, the great concert hall – home that week to the Trades Union Congress – was reduced to ruins. In Trenchard Street houses were damaged, and one completely destroyed.

For safety Fr Thomas Brown hastily carried the Blessed Sacrament from the domestic chapel in Trenchard Street to St Mary's Church, 200 yards away, but although the roof of St Joseph's Hall caught fire and there was intense heat, the absence of any wind that night averted further damage.[1] Across the road from the blazing buildings in Colston Street, an advertising hoarding near the monumental masons just behind St Mary's Church could be seen in the unnatural light. If anyone paused to read in those frantic early hours, it promised comfort of a sort: Red Bell tobacco, it said, could be bought for a little over 1p an ounce, and a trip to London, over 100 miles distant, cost just 25p!

Another, seemingly unconnected, incident had happened a few months earlier. The popular Benedictine priest of Chipping Sodbury, Dr Bernard Sanders,[2] the possessor of a fine voice, was much in demand as a singer. On the evening of May 9, 1898 he was invited to perform at a fund-raising concert at the Colston Hall in aid of the distressed poor in the west of Ireland and had sung a couple of songs when, feeling unwell during the interval, he was forced to retire and was taken by Fr Hulley back to the presbytery in Trenchard Street where he was staying as a guest. He appeared to recover his spirits a little at the supper table, but to the shock of those around him, he suddenly collapsed in his chair and died. The concert was immediately ended.

The death of Fr Edgcome in 1899 – he had been a priest at St Mary's for five years – recalled both occasions. Born in Newcastle he had, at the age of 21, entered the Society of Jesus and been a zealous worker at Glasgow and Liverpool before coming to Bristol, where he was particularly known for his arduous work for the school children and the Boys' Guild. His last work, though he was ill at the time, was the annual retreat for the congregation during Passion Week.

Fr Edgcome, who had been suffering for a considerable time from diabetes, became much worse on the night of April 24 and the two doctors who were called in pronounced that there was very little hope of his recovery. He died at the presbytery in Trenchard Street on the following night, Tuesday, April 25, 1899. "The internal malady to which he succumbed was, it was believed, brought on by the shock which he received at the almost tragic death of the Rev. Dr Sanders, which was accentuated by the disastrous fire at the Colston Hall, during which he worked bravely almost amidst the flames to render assistance to those members of St Mary's whose homes and belongings were threatened with destruction." So wrote the *Bristol Mercury* in reporting his funeral, and continued:

The affection and esteem in which the late Father William Edgcome was held by Catholics in Bristol, and more especially his own congregation at St Mary's on the Quay, were evidenced by the crowded congregation which assembled at St Mary's yesterday morning, when the funeral service was held prior to the interment at Arno's Vale ...[3]

The funeral service, which occupied close upon two hours, opened with the solemn office for the dead, which was sung by the priests. At the solemn requiem Mass which followed, the celebrant was the Bishop of Clifton (Dr Brownlow) ... Mgr Russell, V.G. was the master of the ceremonies, and the Rev. T. Brown, S.J., was the assistant priest at the throne. Dom. V. Corney, O.S.B. was the organist, and the cantors were Father Hulley, S.J. and Father Albert H. Williams.

The Rev. David O'Brien preached an impressive sermon from Eccles. vii, 2: "It is better to go to the house of mourning than to go to the house of feasting, for that is the end of all men and the living will lay it to his heart." He paid a high tribute to the life and work of Father Edgcome ...

After the sermon the solemn dirge was sung by the priests of the diocese, and at the end of the Mass hymns were sung by the children, and Mr Augustus Simmons, the organist at St Mary's, played the "Dead March" from "Saul."

The ceremonies that follow death have their own conventions, interpreted anew by each succeeding generation. In the nineteenth century funeral rites were often richly observed, the period of mourning one to be lingered over. The Victorian funeral has survived as one of the interesting side-scenes of the age and often as the stuff of literature.

In the April sunshine at Fr Edgcome's funeral, large crowds gathered to watch the sombre scene outside the church where eight carriages, with their top-hatted, dark-coated drivers waited to take the officiating priests and numerous clergy to the Catholic cemetery at Arno's Vale. The ceremonial was to continue at the graveside and the first carriage to depart held the acolytes and servers. Twenty-six priests – secular, Jesuit, Benedictine and Franciscan – followed in seven other carriages, and after these came several vehicles carrying private mourners.

The long cortège followed the route of the horse-drawn trams, which had been extended to Arno's Vale only a year earlier. The procession passed over the cobblestones of Bristol Bridge and then by the domed building of E.S. & A. Robinson Ltd, one day to be replaced by Bristol's first office tower. (The funeral some years previously of Mr. E.S. Robinson, a prominent business man and former mayor of the city, had been Victorian on an impressive scale, the mourners following the hearse in 54 carriages.)

As the mourners passed the entrance to the main cemetery they would have seen the lodges flanking the gates, their classical outlines erected in the year that St Mary's was built. In the Catholic cemetery adjoining, Fr Thomas Brown, the Superior at St Mary's, conducted the service at the graveside. The boys and full choir sang the Benedictus, and the hymn for the faithful departed was sung by the school children and guilds who had long been in position for the solemn moment. The *Bristol Mercury* reported that the "coffin consisted of a shell and an outer case of French polished oak with brass furniture, the inscription on the plate being as follows: 'Father Wm. Edgcome, S.J., born 31st August, 1845, died 25th April, 1899.'"

A statue of the Jesuit saint, Francis Xavier, obtained from Munich, was placed in the church in his memory and some time afterwards the parishioners of St Mary's marked the grave, situated a few yards from the chapel wall, with a cross six feet high, inscribed with the initials of the Jesuits' motto: Ad Maiorem Dei Gloriam. Other words at the side show that Thomas Brown, who had led the service of committal and who had been transferred to Manchester in 1901, was himself buried in the same grave ten years later. Now the fiercer sound of the traffic, the television studios smart and confident across the way, and the ivy straggling at the foot of the cross, show the coming of another age.

'Under The Bank', the street on which St Mary's stood, had recently acquired a new name – Colston Avenue. The Council had further adorned the central area with concrete walks and ornamental shrubberies, and erected a bronze statue of Edward Colston, the eighteenth century Bristol philanthropist. The roads on each side were widened.[4] Colston's statue was unveiled by the Mayor, Herbert Ashman, who was himself to receive a signal honour from Queen Victoria, a few weeks after Fr Edgcome's

death: a notice in the London Gazette of June 2, 1899 said that
thenceforth the chief magistrate of Bristol and his successors
would be given the style and title of 'Lord Mayor'; and the
monarch herself was to knight him as he knelt on the carpeted
pavement outside the Council Chamber in Corn Street, beneath
heraldic shields and flags festooning the buildings around.

Another event occurred in 1899 which, though lacking the
gravitas of some important occasions, nevertheless brought quiet
satisfaction to those who took part in it. St Mary's Rugby Club
held its Annual Dinner at the Crown and Dove in Bridewell
Street. Sixty-eight people enjoyed a successful evening for which
the bill amounted to £6.05p.

In that final year of the century there were four priests at St
Mary's – Thomas Brown, Alfred Hulley and (after Fr Edgcome's
death) Joseph Reilly and Stanislaus St John. Masses on Sundays
were at 8, 9.30 and 11 a.m.; Catechism and Benediction were at
3 p.m., and Vespers, sermon, and Benediction at 6.30. Masses on
weekdays were at 7.30 and 8 a.m. On Wednesdays and the first
Friday of the month there was sermon and Benediction at 8 p.m.
The Fathers were also responsible for saying Mass at the Convent
of Our Lady of Mercy, in Dighton Street.

Confessions were heard every morning before Mass and also
on Wednesday evenings after Benediction. Most people took
advantage of the Saturday arrangements when Confessions were
from 2.30 to 4 p.m., and again in the evening from 6.30 until as
late as 10 o'clock.

At the beginning of the nineteenth century there had been one
Catholic church in Bristol – St Joseph's; at its close there were
five: the Pro-Cathedral Church of the Twelve Apostles, St
Bonaventure, St Nicholas, Holy Cross, and St Mary-on-the-Quay.

NOTES

1. "… and he made a solemn offering of twenty Masses for the
preservation of our property." *Letters & Notices*, Vol.27, p.180.
Jesuit Archives, London.
2. "Father Sanders had for several years been on the most cordial
terms with our Fathers in different parts of the country … He was

a great musician as well as being an eloquent preacher, a man of
rare geniality and a most racy raconteur of amusing anecdotes and
witty sayings." *Op. cit.*, p.179, Jesuit Archives, London.

3. Arno's Vale was the first of Bristol's cemeteries, consecrated
by Bishop Monk of Bristol in 1840; next door is the Catholic
cemetery, Holy Souls', opened in 1863; the parish cemetery of St
Mary Redcliffe is opposite. The City Council intends to restore
Arno's Vale, now overgrown.

4. Photographs taken during the last few years of the century
show horse trams passing St Mary-on-the-Quay and horse cabs
available for hire. Women walking along a now-widened Colston
Avenue are wearing long skirts and leg-of-mutton sleeves, and
using umbrellas as sunshades. *Bristol As It Was 1845-1900*, by
Reece Winstone.

CHAPTER 9
A New Era Begins

In 1901, with the death of Queen Victoria and the accession of Edward VII, a new era began. The history of St Mary's from its beginnings to the end of the nineteenth century is the history of a Catholic church in the great Victorian age, a period that saw a growing democratic spirit at home and a trebling of British possessions abroad. Bristol had become a wealthy city, its population growing fivefold over the past century to 328,000 and represented by four Members of Parliament, and although it was no longer second in size to London, by having its chief magistrate raised to the dignity of a Lord Mayor it had been acknowledged as amongst the foremost cities of the kingdom.

And with the introduction of electricity it had become one of the best lighted! But the electric tramway system, which had now reached suburbs as distant as Brislington, Knowle, Kingswood and Bedminster Down, still left the populous city districts of Cotham and Kingsdown, nearer St Mary's, unserved.

At the beginning of the twentieth century the interior appearance of St Mary's was greatly enhanced. The sanctuary was laid with beautiful parquet flooring, and the walls and altar decorated from the designs of the church's architect, Mr Bentley. New sanctuary stalls were installed for the use of the choir (then under the direction of Fr Charles Williams), while in the nave the old benches (antique but not, apparently, attractive) were replaced with new ones and the centre aisle done away with, so providing more space at the sides for processions through the church.

Hitherto the congregation had entered the building through a vestibule "which bore no slight resemblance to a horse-box," and which would have proved a death trap in the event of fire. This was removed, so there was now immediate access to the large doors at the back.[1] And there was another very useful improvement, a new amenity increasingly being enjoyed – electric lighting had been installed.

It was hoped to build a new presbytery adjoining the church, but before he could carry out the plans for this project the architect died, and for many years the work had to be deferred. All this took place during the time that Francis Grene was Superior; he had come to Bristol in 1901.

The highlight for St Mary's in 1903 was the General Mission conducted at the church by Matthew Power S.J. of Edinburgh, assisted by another Jesuit Father, Patrick Power from Dublin. For a whole fortnight the church was packed every night, and on the final evening the colonnade and the street in front were thronged. It was an event that caught the attention of the Catholic national journal *The Tablet*, which remarked on the interest shown by Protestants in the city: "Many of 'our separated brethren', who are noted in Bristol for their strong Catholic sympathies, followed the mission with keen interest, and were given an opportunity of hearing Catholic doctrine preached at the special service which Fr Power has popularised under the name of 'A meeting for Honest Inquirers'."

Some weeks later St Mary's published the number of worshippers attending Sunday Mass at the church since the mission was held:

Morning	8	9.30	11
Easter	267	698	473
Low Sunday	248	553	391
2nd Sunday	139	413	345
3rd Sunday	191	494	408
4th Sunday	192	643	414
5th Sunday	188	520	380
6th Sunday	187	533	428

Encouraging figures one might think, but the Fathers, alert to the dangers of complacency, professed some disappointment: "There is still much room for improvement – much to be desired – if we are to live up to our promises made at the late Mission."

But 1903 was not only the year of the General Mission: May 22 was of special significance for St Mary-on-the-Quay, for it was the hundredth anniversary of the restoration of the English Province of the Society of Jesus.

St Mary's had about half a dozen devotional societies or sodalities[2] (an old Jesuit term) and guilds: Apostleship of Prayer; Men's Sodality; Senior Boys' Guild; Junior Boys' Guild; Children of Mary; Guild of St Agnes; and Guild of St Monica. The Men's Sodality had been newly reconstructed and was 40 strong. In those days, of course, St Mary's had the support of its schools – at Trenchard Street for the boys, and at Dighton Street for the girls. The strength of numbers in the parish was reflected in the attendance at the Children's Tea Party held on January 9, 1903 – 340 boys and girls enjoyed the occasion.

In 1904 Fr Grene estimated that, including the floating population, the number in his parish was around 2,100; one set of figures for attendance at Sunday Mass from Whit Sunday to the fourth Sunday after Pentecost showed 1,201, 1,077, 1,029, 1,158 and 1,081 through the successive Sundays. The average numbers attending Mass on Sundays throughout 1903-1904 were 900 adults and 150 children, and for Sunday Catechism, 175; Easter Communicants numbered 1,356. At Christmas there was Midnight Mass and then Masses every half-hour from 7 to 11 a.m.

The evening services for the four Sundays of the month were, in order: Choral Devotion, Bona Mors, Vespers of Our Lady, and Compline.

The vitality of church life extended beyond formal worship: "The guilds are now complete: all ages of both sexes are well looked after." St Monica's Guild was much encouraged by the Sisters of Mercy in Dighton Street and, although only a year old, soon expected a membership approaching 100. The Apostleship of Prayer was active and had its own Communion day and, at 8 o'clock the same evening, Choral Devotions. St Patrick's Day was always celebrated with a concert, the proceeds of which went to the poor of the parish. Another social event arranged for the 'Sixty Club' or 'The Old Folks at Home' (parishioners over 60 years of age) was attended by 75 people. In 1905 about 70 members of the Men's Sodality (formed at the end of 1903) were present for their annual dinner at the Swiss Restaurant in Baldwin Street, with the Bishop of Clifton as principal guest. There was one exception to this picture of strength – dwindling numbers forced the Guild of St Agnes to close.

Confirmation was administered by Bishop Burton (1902-1931)

on Sunday evening, October 30, 1904 before one of the largest
congregations ever at St Mary's: many could not reach the gates
of the church. One hundred and twenty-seven candidates were
confirmed. Conversions around that time were averaging about 20
a year.

Fr Grene clearly felt the importance of, and interest to be
found in, keeping records, and it was he who made the early
registers of the Bristol mission available for transcribing by the
Catholic Record Society, starting with the first register of
baptisms begun in 1777 by the Jesuit priest, John Fontaine, at the
old chapel in St James's Back, Broadmead.[3]

Fr Grene also had to apply himself to the task of providing
new schools for the boys and girls, whose buildings – the boys'
school next to the church, and the girls' and infants' school in
Dighton Street – had been condemned by the Board of Education
in 1903. They were old, unsanitary, and there was very little
playground. To enable them to be used as temporary schools
certain structural alterations had to be made. A year later, plans
were approved for converting the old St Joseph's Hall in
Trenchard Street into a new boys' school, and for adapting the
old cemetery[4] into a playground, the surface to be asphalted. The
work was completed in 1908 at a cost of between £600 and £700.

In the same year the Managers were required to provide a new
school for the girls and infants, and the difficulty of building a
suitable school on so small a site as the one chosen in Lower
Park Row was finally met by carrying the building on arches, and
utilising the roof as a playground. The building could accommodate 160 girls and 160 infants in classrooms divided by
movable glazed partitions, so that each floor could be used as a
hall. It was an ambitious project costing about £4,500, and
undertaken by the local firm of F. Chown of Montpelier, who
completed it in February 1911.

The new schools were now on adjoining sites. What did the
boys of St Mary's think of the girls, and the girls of the boys?
They were asked to write a short composition giving their views:

Girls are of the female sex. They are not as strong as boys,
though they eat as much as them, especially sugar. They let
their hair grow down their backs, and are very fond of

colour. They all seem to want to wear straw hats and false hair. When it gets dirty they send it to Paxman's to be cleaned. They also dye their hair to make it look pretty and to show off. They get round a boy when he has money and then they go in for jam rolls. Soon after he is stone-broke, and they clear.

Some of the girls were quite perceptive in their comments, but the views of one young lady were decidedly idiosyncratic:

The boy is not an animal, yet they can be heard to a considerable distance. When a boy hollers, he opens his big mouth like frogs; but girls hold their tongue till they are spoken to, and then they are respectable and tell just how it was. A boy thinks himself clever because he can wade where the water is deep. When the boy grows up he is called a husband, and then he stops wading and stays out: but the grown up girl is a widow and keeps house.[5]

During the construction of the new schools, an improvement line for Trenchard Street itself meant that five feet had to be taken off the St Joseph's hall, and the building works generally necessitated disturbing old burial places and dealing with the remains, for the City authorities refused to take over any land containing graves.

Copies of the memorial tablets occupying wall space in the entrance passage were made and the tablets themselves removed to St Mary's in August 1905. There were 44 in all, some commemorating more than one person. Where letters after the name indicated a profession, they showed two captains, three doctors and two priests – six of the seven being under 46 years of age at time of death. In view of the excavations taking place, the Bishop of Clifton was not surprised to receive on December 30 the following somewhat unusual letter from John Bevan of Corn Street, the architect and surveyor:

My Lord Bishop,

<u>St. Mary's on the Quay, New Schools</u>

In setting out the building line and preparing for the foundations, I have come across the bones of:

  Bishop Walmesley who died in 1797,
  Bishop Talbot who died in 1795,
  Bishop Sharrock who died in 1809.

I see no reason why these remains cannot be taken to Downside Abbey, after your Lordship obtains permission from the Home Secretary, as I understand it is the wish of the relatives, as well as the Lord Abbot of Downside.

A week later Bishop Burton applied for a licence for the removal of the remains and this was granted on February 28, 1906 on condition that "the removal be effected with due care and attention to decency, early in the morning." The remains were reinterred in the vault of the Abbey Church, Downside, near Bath. When the yard – the playground of the proposed new school – was lowered, the remains of about 130 persons were discovered and reinterred elsewhere on the site. Other bodies were reinterred in new vaults, one of these containing the remains of the Irish giant Patrick Cotter O'Brien, over 8 feet 3 inches tall according to his memorial plaque. Patrick Cotter, as he was sometimes known, was perhaps the most famous giant in England in his day, a time when giants and dwarfs would display themselves at fairs. He died at the age of 45. His body had been removed from the passage under the steps and found at a depth of about 10 feet below the level of the floor, secure, until then, from all attempts to examine his bones. He had been dead 100 years.

The ordination of the Rev. John Lyons (later to become Monsignor) at St Mary's on Sunday, July 8, 1906 by Bishop Burton was thought to be unique in the annals of the church. The candidate had been born in the parish and had been known to most of the congregation from childhood. Assisting the Bishop at the Pontifical High Mass were Fr Grene and Fr Carolan, and the Master of Ceremonies was the Bishop's Secretary, Fr W.Lee, who became the next Bishop of Clifton.

Figures published for the month revealed that a total of 5,012 people attended Mass on the five Sundays of August that year, an average of 1,002. The averages at each Mass were: 8 a.m. 17%,

9.30 a.m. 44%, and 11 a.m. 39%.

Despite Fr Grene's endeavours, there was one strange deficiency in the church at this time that was left to his successor, Robert Moss, to put right: there was no organ – only a hired harmonium! And although the inventory of 1858 contained a page headed "Gallery", underneath which was the word "Organ", in 1907 Fr Moss arranged for a new organ-loft to be built in the left transept and a new organ provided.[6]

We must not, of course, suppose that St Mary's had been for long without a proper organ: when the church opened in 1843 we were told of "the rich tones of the new and powerful organ," and then in 1860 we learn of quarterly payments being made to the organist, organ-blower, and organ-tuner. And a notice dated October 19, 1887 stated that the organ would be reopened on Sunday, October 30, having been thoroughly repaired after the damage caused by the very hot and dry summer. The repairs had cost £30 and there were to be special collections at Masses to defray the expense. The reality is, of course, that the history of any church speaks continually of repair, redecoration and replacement. And hand in hand with that, the need to raise money.

We have seen that hopes were entertained of building a new presbytery next to the church. What of the one in Trenchard Street? In 1908 Fr Moss found it in a tumble-down state, some of it actually in danger of collapse. A new entrance and new waiting-room were built; extensive repairs were made on all four floors; walls and ceilings were distempered throughout. It was, in effect, patched up and strengthened, with a part of it being rebuilt.

From one of the accounts presented by Alfred Dowling, contractor for all these works, it is possible to see the hourly rates for workers at that time, August 1909:

    Labourer – under 3p an hour
    Mason – under 5p an hour
    Horse, cart and man – under 6p an hour

Money values, of course, were different then.

Fr Moss also, as we have seen elsewhere, continued Fr Grene's efforts to provide new schools for St Mary's boys and girls. The good work continued under Fr George Carolan when, in 1910, Fr Moss left to be Superior at Blackpool.

In those years of fewer social distractions, it was possible to sustain interest in such fund-raising activities as fêtes over a period of several days, and when, in 1912, St Mary's organised one on the Flower Showground at Knowle, now built over, it lasted four afternoons, from July 10 to 13.[7] It was opened by Lady Clare King.

"The object of our appeal," said Father Carolan, "is to free the Mission of a debt incurred through the necessity of altering and rebuilding our schools." It amounted to £2,000. But Fr Carolan had more to say:

> These necessities are not the only ones that demand attention. In our own case there are at least two others.
>   Our church is crying out for redecoration! The present Presbytery is so unsuitable as to be of the nature of a parish scandal! And we have to remember that the tendency of our Congregation is to diminish rather than to increase.

The fête realised £350. The reslating of the church roof proved to be an expensive business, and new benches were provided at a cost of £630; a new pulpit was a gift from one of the Fathers.

The chairman of the Knowle fête was Martin Archer-Shee, active in the life of St Mary-on-the-Quay (he was president of the Men's Sodality) and prominent in the business community of the city as the manager of the branch of the Bank of England in Clare Street. "He is a good fellow but quarrelsome," wrote a correspondent to Fr Brown at St Mary's on one occasion.[8] Within a short time a curious episode was to thrust his family into the public limelight, while the pertinacious Archer-Shee fought to save the honour, as he saw it, of his family's name.

NOTES

1. "... and at the end of the service, when the large doors are thrown open outwards, the priest as he descends the altar-steps can command a fine view of Colston Avenue." *Letters & Notices,*

Vol.27, p.183. Jesuit Archives, London.

2. "As early as 1697 there is a record of a Sodality of St (then Blessed) Stanilaus at Bristol." Note on the parish of St Mary-on-the-Quay, *Clifton Diocesan Directory*, 1955.

3. The first Register is inscribed: "A catalogue of the Christenings performed in the Catholic Congregation of Bristol, Somerset by me, John Fountain, their pastor." *Registers of St Joseph's Chapel, Trenchard Lane [now Street], Bristol 1777-1808*, Catholic Record Society.

4. "The cemetery was private. It was closed in Nov. 1847 (by the Provincial of the Society of Jesus)." *Clifton Visitation Papers (St Joseph's) 1858-59*, Bristol Record Office.

5. These extracts are from the diocesan magazine, *The Messenger*, June 1903, *Bristol Papers*, 22/1/3/4, Jesuit Archives, London.

6. New organ-gallery: *Letters & Notices,* Vol.34, p.231, Jesuit Archives, London.

7. A notice in St Mary's *Fête & Carnival Programme, 1912,* advertised that Bed & Breakfast could be had at the Prince's Hotel, Park Row, Bristol for 15p. *Bristol Papers*, Jesuit Archives, London.

8. "Archer-Shee's letter speaks for itself. He is a good fellow but quarrelsome. Instigated by his wife, he has been a bit vicious." Letter to Fr Brown from "J.G." at Manresa, February 5, 1898, *Bristol Papers*, 20/5/2/2, Jesuit Archives, London.

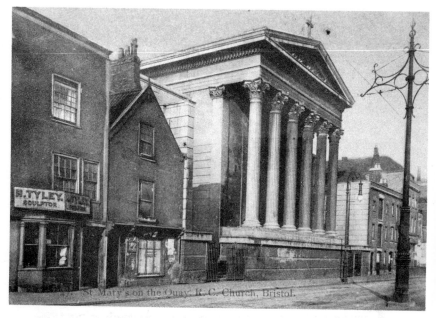

St Mary's on the Quay R. C. Church, Bristol.

The original buildings. The buildings in this picture were the ones that existed in 1843 when St Mary's was opened. By the time of the First World War the two nearest properties had been left to St Mary's. The Tyley family set up as marble masons in Under the Bank (Colston Avenue) many years before the church was built. Henry Tyley ran the business from 1881 to 1925 and then moved to 86 Victoria Street. In the Second World War, the gabled building next to the church was hit by German bombers on the night of Good Friday, 1941. See Chapter 13. (Photo: courtesy Bill Joll)

CHAPTER 10

A Parishioner Remembers

Mrs Mary Harding, who was born in Bristol in the closing years of the nineteenth century and who died in 1983 at the age of 87, was a pupil at St Mary's school when it was next to the church. She recalled some of her memories of St Mary-on-the-Quay:

My parents, Daniel and Charlotte O'Connell, were married by Fr T. Greenan, S.J., and I was born on 31st July, 1896. I started school in the old club-room (next to the church) and was taught by the Misses Clark – known as "Teacher Daisy and Teacher May". There were no chairs, we sat on the wooden stairs, and I remember a little sparrow flying in regularly to eat our lunch crumbs.

One of my first memories of the church was being taken in as a little schoolgirl to see a Fr Thomas Brown lying-in-state in the sanctuary. Also, I remember my father coming home from the St Patrick's Day Mass, with a sprig of shamrock (which had been given to all) stuck to his hair, under his hat – for safety! He was a stone-mason who helped with the building of the Good Shepherd convent at Arno's Vale, and also St Nicholas Church, Lawford's Gate. He remembered the notice for workers required, with the added clause "No Catholic need apply."

When I was five I went to school in Dighton Street, where Miss Manning was headmistress. I remember one of the teachers was Sister Claver, who would rap our knuckles with the edge of a ruler for any rudeness! On her feast day I remember going through the old cellars of the convent to the kitchen to collect pink coconut ice!

Every Monday morning Miss Manning called the register of attendance for Sunday Mass and Catechism – and woe betide those who had not attended *both* services!

In May and June we took part in the processions –

dressed from Miss Manning's stock of over-starched, shapeless white dresses. We wore blue sashes for Our Lady and red for the Sacred Heart. The girls were known by their surnames at school – I remember Edie Brock, Daisy Daly and Nelly Kennealy. The boys were taught by Peter Murphy – a great sportsman. But I remember seeing him cry as he watched the lines of poorly dressed lads go to Communion in ragged trousers and shoes.[1] The boys had no football – they inflated a pig's bladder – 'acquired' from a local butcher!

On Wednesday evenings it was my job to sit in a little space at the side of the church organ, and press the bellows hard for the organist to play for Benediction. We used to wear aprons to school, and I had mine starched especially by a Mrs Brooks on Marlborough Hill – she charged two pence.

In the summer we went by train to Weston for the day, and all had tea in Huntley's Tea Rooms – we had brown and white bread and butter, seed cake and an apple. At Christmas we went to the Prince's Theatre[2] to see the pantomime at the kind invitation of Mrs Macready-Chute who was a Catholic. Mr Chute was the then manager of the theatre. Their son became a Franciscan,[3] and I met him in Rome in 1950. When the Carl Rosa Opera Company came to the Prince's Theatre the soloists sang High Mass at St Mary's.

At that time (pre-1914) there were many wealthy families in the parish connected with the big banks or H.M. Customs and Excise. They sat in the front of the church and paid 'Seat Rents'. The manager at the Bank of England was Mr Archer-Shee. He had a large family and I remember collecting a hamper of children's clothes from his house for distribution at school.[4]

I also remember some of the 'characters' in the congregation – like old Mrs Owens, who hooked two lads out with her crooked umbrella handle because they were talking in Mass! I remember the priests and the wonderful missions, with people queuing along the pavement for admission to the church!

We had Fr Bernard Vaughan – thc 'Society' Jesuit, who appealed to the wealthy for S.V.P. funds, and then slated them for their high living!

Then there were St Mary's own priests – wonderful men. Fr A. Hulley played the violin. He was an asthmatic and he used to pass the time of day with my non-Catholic maternal grandfather. When the old man was dying he was just able to scrawl the word "Hulley" on a piece of paper – and Fr Hulley was there to receive him into the Church.

There was Fr G. Carolan, who took his Irish terrier on his rounds; and Fr D. Lickert, who was so kind to the poor people – and in those days the people were very poor.

When Fr Grene was parish priest, St Mary's became very affluent. He kept a housekeeper, and a valet called Johnny Ray. After a while he was replaced by Fr R. Moss, who economised on everything! All altar boys had to wear white gloves and linen collars – not rubber, in case these were set on fire by the candles. About this time Mary and Nellie Turner came as housekeepers.

My brothers, Pat and Fred O'Connell, were both masters of ceremony and it is strange to reflect that Fred's efforts at repairing St Mary's ceiling single-handed could not stop the present unhappy situation. Long live St Mary's – we have known some marvellous times!

When Mary Harding, who lived at St James's Barton, was taken by her parents to church to see Fr Thomas Brown lying in state it must have been in January 1910 when she would have been 13 years old. The earliest memories that she recalls here are therefore probably those of her schooldays beginning about 1900-1, and they lead us to the First World War when she would have been 18.

We see how close the Church was to people's lives in those days: before the advent of the welfare state it ministered to many and diverse needs (at Christmas the Sisters in Dighton Street would provide food for poor Catholic families). The prejudice against Catholics in the nineteenth century persisted in some quarters into the early part of the twentieth, and achievements were made often in the face of adverse sentiment and conditions.

We see, too, that churchgoers still recognised the practice of 'seat rents', and, for most, Christian names will always be a matter of fashion! The most touching references are, of course, to the poor. And to Peter Murphy, manly in his ways, and – better still – honourable in his tears.

The year 1913 seemed innocent enough. *The Messenger* reported on the school children's tea party: "A really beautiful series of animated pictures was given after the tea. The crowning joy was the Christmas Tree. For the girls, dolls ... for the boys, aeroplanes." All the school children were invited to view the pantomime at the Prince's Theatre. The owners of the theatre, in Park Row, were well-disposed towards St Mary's; they were Catholics and always closed the theatre during Holy Week.

From *The Messenger* of April 1913 we also learn that three months had passed since the benefits of the Insurance Act had come into operation "and the St Mary's Branch of the National Catholic Benefit Society has proved its usefulness by the prompt payment of claims." And in May the weather was idyllic when St Mary's Social Society, accompanied by Fr Carolan and Fr Meyer, visited Cleeve Tea Gardens. "After tea boating on the lake. The homeward return, through Filton, was perfect."

Two months later, perhaps Mary Harding, who had seen King Edward VII and Queen Alexandra when they visited the old Council House in Corn Street, took a penny tram-ride to the Downs to see King George V at the Royal Show, where he reviewed veterans of the Crimean War and the Indian Mutiny. It was a time of peace and these venerable, white-bearded men could speak of battles safely distanced by over half a century. Two years later they were to be called from retirement yet again. Some two dozen of them lined the grass verge of College Green while immediately behind them a group of ladies held aloft a recruiting banner on which the veterans had supposedly written: "We Have Done Our Duty, Come and Do Yours". It was well meant. Patriotism inspires noble, selfless thoughts, and in the sunshine, with stirring music in the air, the flags fluttered proudly. Many onlookers were not then to know that their own loved ones would, in time, fall in the mass slaughter of war and be numbered amongst eight and a half million dead. On the scarred landscape of battle, Death has his own brave show.

NOTES

1. "Sometimes one or more of the boys could not muster a pair of boots to attend Mass but a pair would be found before the next week. Times could be hard then." Letter from a correspondent to *St Mary's Magazine*, May 1967.
2. The Prince's Theatre opened in Park Row in 1867. It was convenient for patrons from the fashionable Clifton district nearby. It was destroyed in the Second World War, 1939-45.
3. Fr Desmond Chute was not a Franciscan but a priest of this diocese living in Italy. He died in 1962.
4. Martin Archer-Shee lost two sons in the First World War. He retired to Woodchester near Stroud.

Yesterday and today. The organ-loft, the Communion rails and the pulpit in the top picture have now gone. The lower photograph shows the sanctuary enlarged to accommodate the free-standing altar. The re-sited organ may be glimpsed bottom right. (Photos: Jesuit Archives; Bill Joll)

CHAPTER 11

The First World War
and Its Aftermath

At the outbreak of the First World War on August 4, 1914, the staff at St Mary-on-the-Quay were Frs George Carolan (Superior), Peter McPhillips, Alfred Hulley, and Cuthbert Meyer, and the times of Sunday services were 8, 9.30 and 11 a.m., and 3 and 6.30 p.m. Although the personnel changed, St Mary's was served throughout the war by four Jesuit priests.

What was the attitude of the Catholic hierarchy to the huge onslaught that Germany launched in Europe? In a Pastoral Letter read to the congregation of St Mary's in the month war was declared, Bishop George Burton denounced German aggression and called for aid for war's victims:

> In this time of peril and distress, when the joint armies of England and Ireland and Scotland are risking their lives on sea and abroad, or are engaged in protecting our coasts at home, against the savage aggression of a would-be Attila, it behoves us all to hasten to the aid of those thousands around us, who are, or who soon may be, the living victims of war's terrible scourge. Poverty and suffering will soon be knocking at thousands of doors: multitudes of women and children, whose husbands and fathers have gone to face death for us who remain at home, may soon be in lack of their daily bread. As you are aware a National Relief Fund has been opened by H.R.H. the Prince of Wales, to which all classes without distinction are gladly contributing; and we are bound not to be behind any section of the community in proving to the world how real is our sympathy for our brethren in want, and how our patriotism is very far from being little more than an idle vaunt.

He then requested that a collection for the Fund be made in all churches and sent to him for handing to the Lord Mayor in the name of the Catholics of Bristol. He concluded:

> We ordain that on that same Sunday, August 30th, there be Exposition of the Most Holy Sacrament in all our Churches and Chapels from the last Mass until the Evening Service; and We exhort the whole of Our Flock to receive Holy Communion on that day, and to pray heartily for the victory of our arms, for the triumph of civilisation and humanity, for the exaltation and prosperity of all peace-loving peoples, for the comfort of the orphan and the widow, and for the alleviation of all distress.
>
> Also it is our wish that as soon as our Schools reopen, the De Profundis be recited morning and evening by our children, until peace is proclaimed, to beg eternal rest for the souls of our fellow Catholics that have fallen for us and with us, fighting by our side, and for the souls of all that from the field of battle have been hurried before the judgement-seat of God.
>
> To all who during the war recite the De Profundis for these objects, either with the Priest after Mass, or at any other time, We grant an Indulgence of Fifty Days.

The commitment of Catholics to the successful prosecution of the war was total, for "The Catholic Church with its civilisation and traditions, stands to lose or gain much by the present war." As expressed by Bishop Burton, the issues were clearly seen as those of right against might, of freedom against oppression, of fidelity to national pledges against their violation, and of the old civilisation of Europe against resurgent barbarism.

The nation was particularly stirred by the plight of Belgium and her people at this time. Thousands of refugees from that country sought asylum in Britain, 2,000 of them being accommodated in Bristol. It was quite common to see Belgian pupils in English Catholic schools.[1] There was, for various reasons, a sentimental attachment to these people and their homeland. The Society of Jesus and many religious houses had historical links with the towns and cities then in the front line of battle, places where, during the days of religious persecution at home, they were able to set up their schools and convents.[2] And it was from Flanders that skilled artisans were asked to come to Bristol in the eighteenth century to work, and whose insistence on freedom to worship as Catholics enabled John Scudamore to set up his chapel in St James's Back.

The congregation at St Mary's was losing familiar faces as men volunteered for the services (conscription was not yet in force), but their place at church was taken by Belgian refugees and Catholic soldiers stationed in the city (the Black Watch Regiment was billeted nearby at the Colston Hall).

There was food rationing. "Eat Less Bread" became a familiar slogan, appearing even on the cliffs of the Avon Gorge, and not only were people urged to consume less bread but it cost more to buy – 3p for a 4lb loaf; butter was 5p, rising as time passed to 7p; sugar remained less than 2p.

Entertainment was restricted too. For the time being there were no excursions or steamboat trips on Bank Holidays. Petrol was increased to just over 4p a gallon and there were few private motor cars to be seen on the roads, though the great majority of people did not, in any any event, own one. Dancing, though, was a pastime that could be pursued without hindrance. Was there not a time, years ago, when it would be proper for a man to put his arm around his partner in the dance only if she were his wife or daughter or sister? Now the Bunny Hug and the Turkey Trot were all the rage. Caught up in the modernity of their age and the changes war brings, young people could only smile in wonderment at days gone by – that such things should ever have been – such shyness! such coyness! such old-fashioned ways!

Masses were said at St Mary's for the safety of our serving men and women, and the Jesuit Fathers exercised a special care for the wounded at the Royal Infirmary. First-hand impressions of war came from the Catholic chaplains, for the most part young men whose manner of speech was coloured by period decency or their school or college ethos:[3] "Our soldiers are most awfully good to German prisoners: the French women cannot understand it. Our lads will treat a wounded prisoner as if he was a pet chicken with a broken leg. You've no idea what good people soldiers are ... My dear Lord, may God save us all and pity us, above all the poor lads He sees smashed and blood-filthy and exiled here: indeed I do not doubt it." Some of these chaplains were killed in France early in the war; others won military honours, such as the Jesuit priest, Fr Francis Donohoe, who was awarded the Military Cross and served as parish priest at St Mary's from 1934 to 1938; he is buried at the Holy Souls' cemetery at Arno's Vale.

Evidence that it was a time of war was all around St Mary's: the Colston Hall was used by the War Office as a recruiting centre, and the Y.M.C.A. building next to it was turned into a canteen for the Forces and called The Dugout. The area outside St Mary-on-the-Quay became a convenient assembly point, and Colston Avenue a familiar thoroughfare for marching feet, whether of the soldiers of the Black Watch or the Glosters, or of the Church Lads' Brigade or hundreds of Sunday School children parading under the banner of the Lord's Day Union.

From January 4, 1915, the city council used the room beneath St Mary's each day between 10.30 a.m. and 3 p.m. for providing school meals (as required under the Education Act), paying rent to the church at the rate of 53p per week.

In the Pastoral Letters delivered by Fr Carolan from the pulpit of St Mary's, Bishop Burton was increasingly strong in his denunciation of the Germans:

> As for the War itself, which is now not merely a defence of justice and right and good faith, but a life-and-death struggle in which we measure our strength with a savage and relentless foe, that loves war for war's sake, it is our duty to aid its prosecution in every way, to pay up cheerfully, to trust our rulers nor be over-critical of them, to aid recruiting, and to beware of those writers and spouters who in the name of a bastard Christianity would call a halt with Prussian Kultur, Pangermanism,[4] and all the spawn of Luther.

The congregation, then, was encouraged to see the war not only as a patriotic struggle, but as a defence of Christian values against a Germanic non-Catholic culture that had gone awry.

In the year in which St Mary-on-the-Quay was built, Queen Victoria had married Prince Albert, whose father was Duke of

Saxe-Coburg, the British royal family thus becoming part of the House of Saxe-Coburg-Gotha. King George V, deciding that his Germanic titles were scarcely suitable at a time of war, adopted the name of Windsor, after the castle, and proclaimed on July 17, 1917: "Our House and the family shall be styled and known as the House and family of Windsor." Through this wartime decision and by the style in which he exercised his role as king, George V enhanced the position of the constitutional monarchy.

Fr Joseph Flynn was parish priest in the last years of the war. He was a very quiet, unassuming man, always warm and helpful and with a gentle sense of humour. For reading he always wore two pairs of spectacles. On one occasion during Mass he had just poured the wine into the chalice and was about to take a little water when the outer spectacles slipped off his nose and headed straight for the chalice. An alert altar boy thrust out his hand and they alighted on his outstretched palm. Without a trace of emotion Fr Flynn replaced them, gravely maintaining his dignity, but afterwards he thanked the young server – and said how much he had enjoyed the look on his face!

Fr Flynn's assistant, Fr Thomas Faulkner, a hard-working priest whose health was never robust, was at one period confined to the presbytery and the same adroit altar boy used to serve at his Mass in the little chapel at the top of the house. After Mass the priest would share with him his cup of tea which always seemed to have been prepared: "That saucerful of tea before leaving for school always seemed like the nectar of the gods to me."

As the war progressed Bishop Burton, in virtue of faculties received from the Pope at the outbreak of hostilities, suspended the laws of Fasting and Abstinence in the diocese: "We hereby dispense, until further notice, from all Fasting and Abstinence, except on Ash Wednesday and Good Friday ... On these two days not only flesh-meat, but eggs and cheese are forbidden to all. Milk and butter are allowed at the chief meal of those who fast, and at all meals of those who do not."

By July 1918, as the Allies crossed the Marne and began their decisive counter-offensive, the turning-point in the war had been reached and Catholics were urged to give thought to the sort of society they wished to live in. Undoubtedly the Bolshevik

Revolution in the east and the shock of events of a catastrophic war had raised in the minds of many the spectre of anarchy and unrest. To enable them to be better informed about social problems and be guided by the right principles, the Catholic Social Guild produced a manual entitled *A Christian Social Crusade* which dealt, from the Catholic standpoint, with such matters as the Living Wage, Housing, Employment, Education, Marriage, and the Family. Catholics were warned from the pulpit to be on their guard against any attack being made upon the sanctity and permanency of the marriage bond. "For wise guidance on a question such as this," said Bishop Burton, "and on many others affecting our attitude to social life, We cannot do better than again recommend the publications of the Catholic Truth Society, particularly its series of *Penny Books on Socialism.*"

A new Code of Canon Law came into force in 1918 and from it the Bishop selected eight changes in the Church's discipline to be mentioned to the Shrove Sunday congregations, mostly on fasting and abstinence, but two concerned Indulgences and the Feast of Corpus Christi:

1. All indulgences are now applicable to the souls in purgatory. Fortnightly confession is sufficient to gain a plenary Indulgence on any day.
2. The Feast of Corpus Christi becomes again a holy day of obligation.

Conscription, which had been introduced in 1916, was extended during the last crucial months of the struggle to include all men up to 48 years of age. Difficulties continued: there was a shortage of margarine; and people naturally complained when the letter-rate was increased to what in today's coinage would be less than 1p. But for many at St Mary's there was better news – the Old Age Pension, which had been 25p and had been increased in 1916 by half as much again, rose on the conclusion of hostilities to 50p. It would not do to sound too grateful, though: "Too little, too late," people wisely said.

Hostilities ceased at 11 a.m. on November 11, 1918. In Bristol the church bells rang, businesses closed and trams and buses came to a halt amidst throngs of jubilant citizens. There was dancing in the streets. At night the celebrations continued and, triumphantly exposed, lights were ablaze.

During the days leading up to the Armistice, the influenza epidemic that was raging in the country had struck Bristol and, in one week in 1918, 197 people died; by January the total of deaths in the city had risen to 1,050, a cruel addition to the ravages of years of war in which, of the 60,000 Bristolians who served their country, 4,000 were killed. St Mary-on-the-Quay produced a special booklet, entitled *Roll of Honour*, in which were written the names of the 545 men of the parish who had joined the forces, many from the same family. There then followed separately the names of the 67 who lost their lives. These records found a more enduring form by way of a fine bronze memorial tablet later fixed to the wall outside the church for passers-by to read.

The first name on this memorial is that of George Archer-Shee. He was the son of Martin Archer-Shee whom we have met previously as a man active and benevolent in his work for St Mary's and prominent in the life of the community. He was manager of the Bank of England's Bristol office and was a member of the city's Education Committee; his wife was one of the managers of St Mary's schools. The family lived over the Bank's premises in Clare Street.

For many years their son, George, served as an altar boy at St Mary's, and he then became a naval cadet at Osborne College on the Isle of Wight. Whilst there he aroused the animosity of a petty officer, perhaps prejudiced against Catholics, who falsely implicated him in the theft of a five shilling postal order and in forging the signature of a fellow cadet. The boy was expelled in disgrace. His father, firmly believing in his son's innocence and determined to save the family honour, secured the services of Sir Edward Carson, the famous advocate (who spent ten days in court for only a minimal fee), and his son was finally exonerated. Sadly he was later killed on active service. The episode, which at the time was something of a *cause célèbre* (the case was discussed in Parliament), was in 1947 to become the subject of Terence Rattigan's play *The Winslow Boy*, well known to theatre-goers and to the public at large through television. Those passers-by,

therefore, who pause before St Mary's war memorial in Colston
Avenue and read the first entry – Archer-Shee G. – are looking
at the name of the real Winslow boy!

Fr Michael King, who had served in the war and arrived at the
presbytery in 1918 in khaki, was parish priest from 1919 to 1924.
He had a genuine interest in history, especially local history, and
his talks on the abbeys and monasteries in and around Bristol
would fill the church.

Over the years St Mary's had expanded, in the sense that it
had acquired a clutch of properties in addition to the church and
the presbytery. For tax purposes the parish Superior was required
to list the buildings and the income derived from their rents:

21 Trenchard Street (Presbytery)		
20 Trenchard Street	. . .	£15
Carpenter's Shop, Trenchard Street	. . .	£20
3 Cotham Road (Springfield House)	. . .	£120
17 Colston Avenue (next to the church)	. . .	£7
15 Colston Avenue	. . .	£24

The shop and house next to the church had been left by William
Heaven, a builder, and 15 Colston Avenue by a Mr Tiley, who
had died in 1914. An attempt to buy Springfield House was made
by its tenant, Mr A. J. Kerry, a Catholic, when he returned from
the war, but it was not a matter that the parish priest felt he could
deal with and it was referred to Farm Street.[5] It was subsequently
sold by Fr King in December 1921. In the meantime the
Trenchard Street presbytery, moving with the times, had acquired
a useful facility – the telephone had been installed!

The growth in the power of the state and the threat this posed
to the freedom and responsibilty of the individual, and to respect
for family life, were issues that Catholics were asked to confront
in the aftermath of war. The rise of a totalitarian communist
power, stretching from its European borders eastwards over a vast
land mass to the Bering Sea and encompassing in its embrace
over two hundred million souls, helped to concentrate and often
polarise thinking on these matters. "Do we need one concrete
instance of this exaggerated view of the powers of the modern
state?" St Mary's worshippers were asked from the pulpit. "We

have it in the clamour of some of our own countrymen for fresh
legislation in the matter of divorce, and in the willingness of the
state to pass such legislation, if sufficiently pressed ... Facilities
for divorce will mean facilities for declension ... [bringing]
trouble into hearts and disorder into families." A petition was
later placed in the church against the proposed measure and
women were urged to sign it.

Unfortunately there is no record of the numbers attending St
Mary's during the war – with the exception of 1915 – but we
have the statistics for this and the post-war years:[6]

	Converts	Easter	Sunday Mass + children	Catechism
1915	24	826	1,015 + 275	260
1919	35	1,302	721 + 277	200
1920	42	1,794	790 + 310	230
1921	27	1,324	996 + 260	190

In peacetime there followed the severe economic problems that
plague a country that has expended its resources in war. St
Mary's congregation inevitably shared in the acute difficulties
facing the city and the nation at large: poverty, high prices and
unemployment. One of St Mary's familes, the McBrides, feeling
that the prefix 'Mc' was a handicap when seeking employment,
simply dropped it from their name; the other side of the family
retained the McBride name with the result that in later years the
Intentions at Masses would sometimes read: "The McBride and
Bride Families". Perhaps Barney McBride, who lived in Dove
Street for a time, found fortune in the New World, for many
years later when St Mary's was threatened with closure he wrote
from Canada offering a generous donation to any fund for saving
the church.

For a number of years in the 1920s, 10% of the insured
workforce in the city had no job. It was a measure of the distress
of the times that in 1921 the city authorities distributed to the
needy 315 tons of coal and 4,300 pairs of boots, and in
succeeding years at Christmas-time continued to assist the poor.

When a country is experiencing such problems, the
mismanagement of the nation's affairs by the government, and by

the Chancellor of the Exchequer in particular, is the conventional wisdom by way of explanation. In 1921 Bishop Burton saw things differently. Looking beyond the details of the present and seeking a profounder cause, he surveyed the centuries past and found it in the Reformation and the subsequent growth of Protestantism and its secular ally, the capitalist State:

> Where, too, shall we discover, in greatest part, the true roots
> of our present ever recurring economic troubles except in
> the rise of Protestantism, that essentially aristocratic
> movement, which in our land enriched itself with the
> plunder of the Church, and, after reducing the monarchy to
> impotence, built for itself an industrial and capitalist State?

In the same year the Holy Father, moved by the plight of Russia's starving millions, asked that a collection be made in the churches to help relieve their distress. "It is a country which would seem to have had enough of Communism," observed the Bishop to his flock. Alas! not for another 70 years.

NOTES

1. "By June 1916 some 140 Belgian boys were in attendance at Wimbledon College [London] – probably a record number for refugees at any English school." *The Jesuits in England* by Francis Edwards S.J., 1985, p.228.
2. "But most of those [English Jesuits] who were not missionaries in England and Wales lived and worked in the English houses in the Low Countries. These were at Watten in France ... at Liège ... and at Ghent. Perhaps the best known of the English Jesuit houses was the College at Saint-Omer ... it was compelled in 1762 to leave what had become French territory and it settled at Bruges." *William Strickland and the Suppressed Jesuits* by Geoffrey Holt S.J., 1988.
3. At Campion House, Osterley, in 1916, Edmund Lester S.J. founded the Knights of the Blessed Sacrament. "Its atmosphere recalled something of mediaeval chivalry in promoting devotion to the Eucharist. Its success showed that even if the age of

chivalry was past the knightly ideal could still attract youthful imagination even in the twentieth century; and even in a modern army. The Redemptorists and others shared the labour of spreading the devotion which had considerable success among Catholic soldiers in the first world war." Francis Edwards, *op. cit.*, p.222.

4. 'Pangermanism': Pan-Germanism. The Pan-German League was founded in 1891 and preached extreme nationalism in home and foreign affairs. After the First World War its activities declined, but Hitler's National Socialist party adopted its political theories.

5. Farm Street Church (or Mount Street) is the name popularly given to the church of the Jesuit Fathers in the Mayfair district of London, their first London church, opened in 1849 under the title of the Immaculate Conception. The site was originally part of Hay Hill Farm which in the eighteenth century extended beyond Berkeley Square. Fr Randal Lythgoe, who laid the foundation stone in 1844, was the Provincial who negotiated with Bishop Ullathorne and Fr O'Farrell in 1847, when it was proposed that the Jesuits should take over St Mary's.

Farm Street is the road to the front of the church and Mount Street – in which the Jesuits have their residence, adjoining the church – to the rear.

6. *Diocesan Statistics 1902-1933*, Clifton Diocesan Archives.

Miss Catherine Manning. (Photo: courtesy Bill Joll)

CHAPTER 12

Miss Manning and Mr Murphy

When thinking about her schooldays at St Mary's in the early 1900s, Mary Harding had clear memories of her headmistress, Catherine Manning, and of the headmaster of the boys' school, Peter Murphy. They were teachers of influence who held their posts for many years and about whom former pupils were disposed to use the term 'legendary'.

Catherine Manning came to Bristol at the turn of the century and was appointed headmistress of St Mary's Girls' School in Dighton Street when still only 24 years of age. She took lodgings at the home of the Russell family at 10 Myrtle Road, on the slopes of Kingsdown above St Mary's church. Although Mr and Mrs Russell were members of the Church of England, the young Miss Manning's influence was such that as each of their children was born (they had two daughters and six sons) it was agreed that she would take the child to St Mary's to have it baptised a Catholic. In this way over a period of 11 years, during the rectorships at St Mary's of Fr Moss, Fr Grene and Fr Carolan, seven of the children became Catholics.

One of the sons, Francis Russell, takes up the story:

> From time to time Miss Manning would invite the parish priest to tea giving them a chance to discuss school and parish business. This meant a family blessing as he was leaving. When the new schools were opened at Lower Park Row in 1911, the boys, girls and infants became a much closer school combination. During this period Miss Manning did outdoor collecting in common with many others, going through the streets of St Augustine's, Wells Street, College Street and those little streets that stood where the Council House now stands.[1]

Each year had its seasonal jobs. The Lenten period was a time when Miss Manning (and all the other teachers of course) stressed to her girls the importance of Confession and Communion, encouraging them to go weekly if possible. To this end she would make a cup of tea for any girl who had been to Mass and Communion before school. Easter also meant First Communion for many children. The girls and infants would assemble at the school so that Miss O'Reilly and Miss Manning could check them, adjust dresses and ribbons, and line them in procession with the older and taller girls at the back, as many as possible with veils. The procession would walk from Lower Park Row to the church, being much admired by onlookers in an age when Catholics were not accepted as they are today. After the Mass the children were walked to the convent in Dighton Street for their traditional First Communion Breakfast. This was always a very happy occasion.

From the opening of the new schools until her retirement, Miss Manning ran whist drives with great success. When the drive started I would stay behind to help with the refreshments. Coffee was made by the Misses Turner, housekeepers [at the presbytery] for so many years and so capable. It would be carried in large white jugs from their kitchen across the garden, up the wooden staircase, across the school playground and into the school. Quite a long walk in the dark and sometimes in wet weather. The drives were always held on Fridays so that Saturday mornings were a sort of 'restoration day', everything being put ready for Monday's lessons.

Another great event was the jumble sales. With her many connections and friends Miss Manning was never short of an address to send us to for collections. Shopkeepers, individuals and the Prince's Theatre all had to be visited and we would bring back what seemed to us an Aladdin's Cave of treasures. When the things were being sorted, Miss Manning would set aside any article of clothing which she knew one of her girls would find handy. These items were distributed as soon as they arrived so that no one knew they were from the jumble sale.

Another job that Miss Manning helped with was the Parish Magazine. My brother and I were very gently persuaded every month to stand on the church steps on the first Saturday evening from seven till nine and on the Sunday morning and evening to try and sell every book we had![2] This we did until we became altar boys.

There are still some who remember the May and June Processions, which sometimes left the church, walked around the front of it and back to the altar again. What a beautiful sight it was with the infants and older girls in their white dresses and veils, gathered together by Miss O'Reilly and Miss Manning. They were then handed over to the Nuns who always seemed to get them into a perfectly graduated column.

In mid-1927 Miss Manning's health began to give cause for concern. She consulted a surgeon friend and after a very prolonged investigation she was told she had cancer – with six months to live at the most. Armed with her faith she set about the task of preparing for her death. She had a short holiday with her only relative, her niece, visited one or two friends then returned home.

By the end of August she had taken to her bed. Her expressed wish was that we would play whist with her each evening. This was only interrupted when visitors called. Many ex-scholars came to see her, yet her consideration of their welfare was such that she always insisted I escort them through the dark streets which is what I did as far as they wished. She played cards right to the end even though the pain was so great. Sometimes we would wait a moment until she could gather her mind together for the card to play.

The end came on 21st January, 1928. At the age of 54 years, Catherine Manning, winner of souls went, I am sure, to claim a just reward. Even after her death, her care for others showed itself. The night before she died, she said to my mother: "I will not be here to wish Francis a Happy Birthday, so will you please give him this envelope." That was a typical Catherine Manning act, helping others until the day of her death.

The endeavours of Peter Murphy, Headmaster of the Boys' School seemed to say: I must make every boy a good citizen. It was said that no boy ever left school with a poor character reference. He was able to find some good points and managed to omit the less favourable ones. It must have been difficult with some whose mental abilities were limited.

Another good asset was his ability to join the boys in the playground, playing cricket and showing them the art of bowling, making the ball do all sorts of odd movements. We boys were always spellbound. However, music was his great love and his contributions in this field, certainly to the church and school, were tremendous. His singing lessons at school were always enjoyed and on the occasions of a visit by the school inspector, or any visitor of note, we would duly perform for their benefit.

From school to church – here again his influence with the choir, gathering round him the very best of local singing talent. His leading soprano was Miss Edith Brock, a popular teacher with Miss Manning. Her singing was quite effortless – the tone clear and sweet as anyone could wish to hear. Her solo part in the Mass and her "Come to the Manger" solo at Christmas were a joy to hear. Another 'local' who joined the choir as soon as she was able, was Peggy O'Gorman. Her very strong contralto voice enriched the choir and gave it that little extra fullness so often missing in small choirs.

There were other singers of note, but these two ladies were the 'Jewels in the Crown'. They were ably supported and their voices enhanced by a very accomplished organist at that time, Jimmy Fitzgerald. His interpretations of those hymns intended to stir the mind, such as Faith of our Fathers, were excellent. He made one feel one must take up arms and fight for the Church, in spite of danger, fire and sword. However, there is the sad time when one loses a dear one or the church loses one of its very own, and also Remembrance Day when we all remember those who died for us. So moving was our organist's rendering of the Dead March in Saul that there was hardly a dry eye in church by the final note, the silence broken only by the emotion being shown.

Peter Murphy (left) and St Mary's School rugby team, 1920. St Mary's Rugby Club is one of the oldest in the city and over the years has supplied several players to the Bristol team. The Bristol Catholic Skittles League – of which St Mary's players are active members – is, perhaps, unique. Is there another such Catholic league elsewhere? (Photo: courtesy Bill Joll)

Peter Murphy, indeed, had a very accomplished choir. Professional singers from the opera companies when visiting Bristol's two theatres would always join the choir for the morning Mass and evening service. The McCready-Chutes who managed the Prince's Theatre were noted parishioners so it followed that anyone who could sing was directed to St Mary's.

About 1923 Peter Murphy retired. Miss Manning was very involved in arranging a farewell evening. It was very well attended, many parents and old boys coming to bid farewell to this warm-hearted and respected headmaster who, I believe, had served them well for twenty-eight years. At the close of the evening he was asked to sing and he chose 'Love's Old Sweet Song'. With his rich baritone voice he gave a rendering that held his audience in utter silence, but hankies were very evident among the ladies. He was obviously moved himself and paused once or twice during his speech of thanks after the long applause had died down.

This was a sad time for St Mary's. With his retirement as headmaster so came his retirement as choirmaster, an office which proved much more difficult to fill. Eventually things settled and life went on as before.

NOTES

1. Many Catholics lived in this area.
2. This was *The Messenger*, which contained a supplement of news from the various parishes, tending to make it thicker than a normal magazine – thus the reference, no doubt, to "book".

CHAPTER 13

St Mary's before Vatican II

Fr Cuthbert Meyer had been a priest at St Mary's both before and after the First World War. He was an assistant priest from 1911 to 1915, before joining the Forces as a military chaplain; during service in Egypt he was mentioned in dispatches. He was reappointed to St Mary's in 1919 and became parish priest in 1924.

By 1933, then aged 64, he was in indifferent health but the Provincial, Fr Harry Keane, was having difficulty finding a suitable replacement. There followed, during the period from November 1933 to September of the following year, correspondence between the Bishop and the Society on possible solutions to the situation at St Mary's. At one stage Bishop Lee offered to find staff himself, but the Provincial felt the Society itself could yet resolve the matter: "Our Fr General has given the matter careful consideration and ... it has seemed to him not altogether wise that we should leave so promising a field as Bristol."[1]

In 1934 Fr Meyer became Spiritual Adviser at Beaumont College and was succeeded at St Mary's by Fr Francis Donohoe, a genial northerner, a man of charm and simple humility who, like Fr Meyer, had distinguished himself in the First World War. On his appointment as a military chaplain in 1917 he had left Liverpool, where he had been teaching, for France and served with the Royal Irish Fusiliers. He was awarded the Military Cross in 1918 and later the Belgium *Croix de Guerre*; he was also mentioned in dispatches.

At St Mary's he found there was much to be done: a debt of £3,000 had accumulated – a considerable sum in those days – and the interior of the church was exceedingly drab. One of his first tasks was to gather around him a band of loyal workers who, in the days before the now familiar name of parish committee, took the title of the St Mary-on-the-Quay Entertainment Committee;

Vincent Dimambro was elected its first secretary. Recalling the overall situation in those days, Vincent later commented: "Altogether it seemed that a dark cloud hovered over St Mary's."

The committee set to work to establish social and fund-raising events. A good social atmosphere was built up through holding dances, which were initially all-ticket events but became so successful that they were held regularly on Friday nights. Contemporaries noted that quite a few marriages followed from the friendships formed! Bishop Lee was anxious to help the church and willingly accepted invitations to attend fund-raising events.

In 1937 a letter to Fr Donohoe from Fr John Luck, who formerly served at St Mary's, reveals one of Fr Donohoe's interests at that time:

> I am so glad that you are taking an interest in the ancient
> churches of Bristol. It will repay you, for you are living in a
> treasury of antiquities, perhaps the richest in England, for I
> believe there were more churches within the same space
> than anywhere else – about twenty-five within the walls ...
> and ten or twelve outside.[2]

In the years immediately before the Second World War, the strength of the parish was such that the committee could confidently organise pantomimes that could play to crowded and enthusiastic audiences in the church hall for several days or even a full week.

Fr Donohoe then suggested that St Mary's should hold Sunday evening concerts like those in the Catholic parishes of Lancashire where he had previously served. Such Sunday night events were hitherto unheard of at St Mary's, where the committee regarded it as a rather daring idea needing careful investigation. Would, for instance, the local police have any objection? None was raised, so the committee set about promoting St Mary's first Sunday evening concert.

There was a great deal of talent in the parish in those days – or available to the organisers from non-Catholic friends who always responded well to their appeals for support. The concerts were so popular that queues frequently formed outside the church hall before the doors were opened, and the committee had to devise ways to allow prior access to people who had attended the evening service. The admission charge, 3p, was for entertainment that lasted at least one and a half hours.

During this successful period a sad event occurred. In 1938, following an accident he had at the presbytery, Fr Donahoe was confined to bed with thrombosis. Despite his serious illness, visitors were impressed with the cheerfulness he unfailingly showed. His successor, Fr Joseph Doyle, said of him: "He was truly a man of God. He lived a life of intense prayer and under him the parish was spiritually rejuvenated." Fr Donohoe was buried at the Holy Souls' cemetery, Arno's Vale, next to the grave of Fr Edgcome.

The impression he made on those who knew him may be judged from a letter that the parish priest at St Mary's received almost 40 years later from a correspondent in Dublin. The letter, dated August 26, 1975, read:

> I have suddenly realised that Fr Frances Donohoe was born at Wigan on this day 99 years ago. I have had his photo in my pocket for the past 40 years and continue to think of him as still 62 years old ... He was (and is) a very great friend of ours all over the years and visited us in Dublin. My brothers and myself and my sons were all at school with the Jesuits in Dublin and they have been very good friends of ours for the past 70 years. If someone could produce a picture of Fr Donohoe's grave at Arno's Vale I would be very grateful.[3]

One Friday evening early in January 1939, Cecil Goodway, one of the altar staff at St Mary's, was passing through the church (a service was shortly to take place) when he was startled to see the large Crib at Bethlehem, which had been set up in the Sacred Heart chapel as part of the Christmas celebrations, ablaze. Within minutes of the alarm being raised, two crews of firemen had manned their engines and were racing to the scene.

The dozen or so firemen found the church full of smoke, and flames now menacing the altar of the Sacred Heart in the north transept. Using a small hose and working by the lights of the church, they soon extinguished the fire so that the damage was confined to a small section. The altar had suffered and the crib had been completely destroyed. The walls of the chapel were blackened and disfigured, while the organ loft directly above was scorched but otherwise undamaged. When they had made all safe, the firemen returned to base and quickly resumed what they had been forced to abandon – some had been enjoying their annual party and others had been taking part in a whist drive! The parish priest thought the cause of the fire was probably a lighted candle falling over or a gust of wind spreading its flame.

The war years were to intervene but in December 1951 the Sacred Heart altar was replaced and dedicated to the memory of Fr Francis Donohoe. A new statue for the altar was sculpted by the well-known London artist, Atri Brown, but it met with little approval by St Mary's congregation and was replaced in 1965 by a beautiful statue of the Sacred Heart of Jesus which had been carved in Carrara, in northern Italy. This was a generous gift of Bristol's Italian community.[4]

Almost eight months after the fire, an event occurred that was to affect the lives of millions. The news of it was broken to St Mary's congregation from the pulpit by Fr Doyle on September 3, 1939 at around 11.15 a.m. when, after reading the notices and the banns of marriage, he reported the message broadcast minutes earlier by Neville Chamberlain, the prime minister: the country was at war with Germany.

The signposts in the centre of Bristol pointed in different directions but the message they bore was the same – that air-raid shelters could be found close by. Soon after the outbreak of the Second World War in 1939, there were shelters in the vicinity of St Mary-on-the-Quay for 4,310 people; seven years later those erected opposite the church, in Magpie Park, had still not been removed, though hostilities had ceased some 12 months previously. In the aftermath of war there were other priorities.

One of the Sunday night series of concerts introduced in Fr Donohoe's time provided the background to the first dramatic war-time experience for many of the St Mary's congregation. During the night of November 24, 1940, the first of the bombing raids on Bristol took place. Flares dropped by German planes lit up the night sky as people, many of them children accompanied by their parents, crossed the Tramways Centre and arrived at the parish hall in Colston Avenue for the customary Sunday concert; they were compelled instead to take shelter in the adjoining crypt. Shortly the thud of bombs could be heard. While older people were anxiously thinking of relatives and friends elsewhere in the city, the younger ones were soon singing to the music played by some of the artistes. Later a few of the boys and girls left their shelter and went upstairs to the canteen to bring refreshments down to the crypt. In such ways people occupied themselves and remained cheerful through the long hours as high explosive and incendiary bombs laid waste areas of the city, some but a short distance away.

When the all-clear sounded and people were able to go outside, they gazed in amazement at the scene before them: it seemed as though the whole city was ablaze. Immediately across from the church it was as though a bomb had hit Magpie Park, in the centre of Colston Avenue, and in the gaping hole the waters of the river Frome, hidden since 1893, gleamed in the fires of the night. What seemed a tangle of hosepipes criss-crossed the street. Many of the people leaving St Mary's could reach their homes only by making long detours and, as they travelled the wasted city streets, they became increasingly aware of the devastation of the German raid. But none of those who sheltered in the crypt was injured or had his home destroyed in this, the first blitz on Bristol.

With so many artistes away on war service, it became impossible to organise Sunday concerts as before, so James Fionda, St Mary's organist, offered to run film shows instead. It proved to be a popular form of entertainment and a useful way of adding to the fund Fr Doyle, the parish priest, launched for redecorating the church; some hundreds of pounds were raised in this way. Towards the end the biggest problem was in obtaining new films.

The parish priest had the additional task of organising fire-watching parties, which were ably led by Fr Lawrence Crehan. On one occasion there was a deafening noise and the lights went out as an incendiary crashed through the skylight of the sacristy, landing on the vestment press. Fr William Lawson, a Jesuit temporarily assisting at St Mary's, and a fellow fire-watcher manoeuvred the bomb onto the floor where they extinguished it; the vestments were saved but the priest's biretta perished in the attack! They then dealt with more incendiaries in the top clubroom before finally taking refuge in the school shelter. Apart from this, although because of its position it was at the centre of all air raids on Bristol, St Mary's was virtually untouched.

During the attack by German bombers on Good Friday, April 11/12, 1941, Fr Anthony d'Andria was outside the church firewatching with Dan Newport, a member of the congregation, together with an employee of Abrahams' glass and china warehouse next to the church, a building owned by St Mary's. The raid was at its height and the noise of bombing and anti-aircraft fire intense when the priest suddenly cried out: "We must save the Blessed Sacrament!" and with his companion rushed into the church, momentarily forgetting it was no longer there, the day being Good Friday. On going outside again they were shocked to discover that the warehouse had been struck and, sadly, the employee killed. On the other side of the church and next to it the *Evening World* building was damaged, John Wright's printing works were burning and the insurance offices in Zed Alley reduced to rubble. As wave after wave of planes attacked the city that night, 180 people were killed. It was the sixth and last large-scale attack on Bristol.

Fr Doyle soon lost the services of Fr Weatherhead, who joined the Forces as a chaplain, and he no longer had the assistance of his choir master, Frank Duggan, who was on military service abroad; but with the aid of senior choristers he kept the choir together, and boys from St Brendan's College, the Christian Brothers' school, lent support.

Although the St Mary's centenary anniversary in 1943 fell in the middle of the war years, it was observed in fitting fashion. Bishop William Lee, using the same crozier as was carried by his predecessor, Bishop Baines, a century earlier, presided at a dignified and colourful ceremony and was present again at Benediction in the evening. Flowers adorned the sanctuary and at each service the church was overcrowded.

It was decided, at Fr Doyle's suggestion, to commemorate the occasion by commissioning the design and creation of a Centenary Monstrance, and to this end a Presentation Fund was established to which people contributed precious metals and jewellery to be embodied in the finished work. Its completion was delayed by the war and by the ill-health of the artist, H.W. Greatrex of Birmingham, for it was hand-beaten throughout, and it was not until January 1953 that the finished monstrance was handed over to the church. Modelled upon the throne in St Mary-on-the-Quay it is of solid silver, surmounted by a cross of pure gold, carrying rubies and diamonds. The creator considered it his masterpiece.

Towards the end of the war the whist drives held at St Mary's proved to be so popular that tables were set up not only in the hall but in the adjoining crypt to accommodate the two to three hundred patrons who regularly attended. One evening the enthusiastic organiser, the diminutive Vincent Dimambro, was confronted by two burly police officers who told him the hall was grossly overcrowded and the crypt entirely unsatisfactory for such purposes. Although he could no longer use the crypt and was compelled to reduce the number of tables to 40, the indefatigable Vincent continued to run his whist drives (a great attraction to Catholics and non-Catholics alike) for three evenings a week, and raised thousands of pounds for St Mary's.

The master of ceremonies at this time was Frederick O'Connell, one of the most distinguished holders of this position at St Mary-on-the-Quay. He was in charge of an altar staff of some 20 or more servers, their numbers being such that they would line up in twos around the large outer sacristy prior to processing into the church. He offered, single-handed, to clean the interior of the church, including the three pictures on the back wall of the gallery whose canvases had darkened with the years, and succeeded in revealing the colourful pictures beneath the grime, though regretfully as time passed they deteriorated again.

Because of his imposing height it was customary, during the times when there was a large altar staff, for Joseph Doolan to lead the procession as Cross Bearer. Joseph was another of St Mary's long-serving parishioners; he had joined the altar staff at nine years of age, when Fr Cuthbert Meyer was parish priest, and continued as a server until his death in 1992, 65 years later.

At the end of the war the exterior of the church was cleaned and, at the instigation of Fr Doyle, the inscription *Vivat Christus Rex*[5] was cut above the beautiful cream-coloured pillars of the portico in commemoration of the establishment by Pope Pius XI of the feast of Christ the King. Fr Doyle had himself been present at this great event in St Peter's, Rome.

The ordination at St Mary's in 1948 of Fr Terence Corrigan, a Bristol man, proved to be a particularly happy and significant event, for in time this young Jesuit priest became Provincial of the English Province of the Society of Jesus, and was a visitor to St Mary's in that capacity.

The liturgy at St Mary's attained a high standard in those days, and with Jimmy Fionda and Frank Duggan in charge of the music the enthusiasm and discipline amongst the choristers was such that the men used to sing Compline before their weekly choir practice.

In 1951 Mr H.S. Goodhart-Rendall, former President of the Royal Institute of British Architects, was commissioned to design and carry out the complete interior redecoration of St Mary's, but while the scaffolding was still in the process of being erected Fr Doyle received instructions to leave Bristol, where he had been for 13 years, and serve at the church of The Holy Name, Manchester.

One Sunday afternoon 23 years later, in 1974, an elderly figure could be seen crossing the sanctuary of St Aloysius' Church, Oxford – it was that of the redoubtable Fr Joseph Doyle, then 83 years of age, who had come to St Mary's in late 1934 and remained to be parish priest from 1938 to 1951. Afterwards he had kept in touch and had revisited Bristol in recent years; now he was talking enthusiastically about visiting Rome again. That particular Sunday afternoon, he had administered one baptism and was preparing for another, when he suddenly slumped beside the pulpit and shortly afterwards died.

The Requiem Mass at St Aloysius four days later on November 21, concelebrated by the Auxiliary Bishop of Birmingham and the Deputy Provincial of the English Order of the Society of Jesus, was attended by many people from Bristol. At St Mary's own Requiem for him the tribute Fr Vincent Norbury paid gives a fascinating picture of Catholic life before the Second Vatican Council:

Sometimes we can discern how the life of a particular person can epitomise the spirit of a particular age. For us at St Mary's, Fr Doyle epitomises the Church prior to Vatican II.

But it was a Church set in a different pattern from our modern Church. The last Mass of the day in those days was at 11 a.m. The Sunday School in the afternoon and Evening Service completed the worship of the day. The Church then was a non-television Church. Ecumenism hadn't come on to the Catholic scene. There was a neatness and simplicity about the pastoral routine. One was concerned firstly and lastly with the flock, one's own parish, and not too bothered with concerns outside it. Those concerns were looked after by other authorities. Pastoral or parish councils had not come on to the scene. The People of God was not a household term nor had its responsibilties become activated. In that setting Fr Doyle grew in a well-defined and predictable role and, during the 17 years he was here, dominated the life of the parish.

Those were the days of the convert as these are not and in our Jesuit Society he became the best-known instructor where his zeal and ability were outstanding. They were the days of the parish school as these are not; and Fr Doyle was a daily visitor and shared a good deal of his daily life with the teaching staff and children. He became the focal point around whom the parish turned – children, parents, teachers – those whose needs were never adequately supplied at that time by the Social Services, by Education authorities, by the visual aids of television, by the tape and cassette. Instead people turned readily to their parish priest and Fr Doyle rose to the challenge, never sparing himself, always trying to relieve the many needs of the people under his care.

There were other characteristics too of Fr Doyle we might refer to. He had an inflexible loyalty to the Holy See

which accepted without criticism whatever instructions
issued forth. Criticism of any kind to the Holy See, to the
Hierarchy, to the Bishop, was not only an act of disloyalty:
it was an offence gainst the Faith itself. The liturgy, the
centre of worship and the centre of the life of the parish
was to have special emphasis and interpretation.
Concentration was duly given to the Children's Mass where
children, teachers and parents filled the church each Sunday
at 9.30 and where community was truly built up. There was
a deep satisfaction at seeing the children, the younger and
older ones, gradually finding their place, or as we say today,
being integrated into the larger community of the parish.

The 11 a.m. Mass was the time for the Liturgy of the
High Mass where action was solemn, slow, dignified,
completely expressed in Latin said or sung. Acolytes and
Thurifer and Torchbearers, as well as Deacons and
sub-Deacons with humeral veil were fully used and
generations of young people were laboriously taught their
parts as well as their Latin. And the sermon was long,
always long. Fr Doyle lived this liturgy and relished it and
it inspired his congregation to participate by what was then
the normal channel for participation – by singing, glorious,
joyful and happy singing of the Latin chants and the hymns
of the Mass with which one had grown up from schooldays
and become nostalgically familiar. Fr Doyle was truly the
High Priest of the Liturgy and the congregation under his
encouragement became outstanding in its singing role.

The other virtue of the very many that he rejoiced in and
by which he became exemplary as a priest of his day was –
in seeking for a name for it I can only use the term
Fatherliness. He was always Father Doyle and no cheap use
of his Christian name, by his contemporaries and much less
by any member of the congregation was acceptable to him.
His Fatherliness belonged to his very nature and was
expressed in his every attitude of concern and availability.
He was concerned for every member of his parish and his
concern was a fatherly concern, a never ending one, a
concern that was always seeking and trying to promote their
good. When he was away, even after leaving the parish, he

continued his concern with the writing of letters, with the readiness to visit when the opportunity arose. Today we are inclined to resent paternalism but we would be very wrong to mistake this for what we all need – a true fatherliness is always concerned for our best interests, always encouraging and supporting. Fr Doyle seemed to have this in an eminent way ...

If we asked him perhaps he would urge us to love our Church and our Faith with a total and unqualified dedication and then express it in ways appropriate and relevant to our own times. Then we might well approach death as he did undaunted and unassuming, fully immersed, engaged in complete involvement with that ministry the good Lord has assigned to each one of us.

NOTES

1. Correspondence between Bishop Lee and the Provincial on staffing at St Mary's, 1933-34. The correspondence ended on September 22, 1934 with a letter from the Provincial, Joseph Bolland: "My one desire is to give your Lordship as zealous and energetic a team as I can at St Mary's." Clifton Diocesan Archives.
2. *Bristol Papers*, 20/5/4/2, Jesuit Archives, London.
3. The photograph was sent.
4. Atri Brown's statue was well received by the church of Our Lady and St Alphege, Bath.
5. The words were produced from an original design by Fr Francis Grimshaw when he was at St Joseph's, Fishponds, Bristol. He later became Archbishop of Birmingham.

Miss Nellie Turner. She and her sister, Mary, came from Lancashire in 1907 to be housekeepers at the presbytery in Trenchard Street. They served for 47 years. (Photo: Jesuit Archives)

CHAPTER 14

The Post-War Years

In the years following the Second World War there was, inevitably, a severe shortage of housing, and an earlier generation accustomed to finding rented homes without difficulty was succeeded by another which found accommodation scarce and expensive, and house prices now expressed in thousands of pounds instead of, as formerly, in hundreds. St Mary's Magazine was not infrequently used by members of the congregation requesting flats or accommodation to rent.

Fr Doyle had been succeeded by Fr Lawrence Crehan (a trained pharmacist), a kindly man with a keen social conscience, who was particularly at ease with young people. He was an inveterate smoker!

Under him the guilds and sodalities still operated successfully. In the early 1950s the Guild of St Stephen, the Children of Mary, the Society of St Vincent de Paul, the Agnesians, the Union of Catholic Mothers, and the Men's and Women's Sodalities were all to be found at St Mary's. For some of the associations it was customary to go to Communion monthly in a body; they often organised visits. The Junior Altar Staff too were in sufficient strength to have their own outings. The Men's Sodality held well-attended Retreats. So it was that the Jesuits' Director-General of the Sodalities in England could speak of "an excellent spirit" in the sodalities when he visited St Mary's in 1952.

For two weeks in March 1953, a mission was conducted at St Mary's led by Fr Bernard Farrell of the Society of Jesus and Fr Gardiner Gibson, an American Jesuit who was in England for a year's study. One of St Mary's oldest parishioners at the time said he could not recall the church being so consistently full as it was during this fortnight when the two missioners preached. Bishop Rudderham (who had been appointed in 1949) gave Solemn Benediction on the closing night and all available space (including the sanctuary) was used to accommodate worshippers;

even so, there was an overflow congregation in the parish hall to whom the service was relayed.

Four distinguished St Mary's people retired in 1954. Mr James Barnidge had been headmaster at the boys' school since 1925 and was in overall charge of the Catholic children of the area when they were evacuated to Exmouth during the war. Mrs Kathleen Pennington had, in a quiet but sure manner, proved to be a worthy successor to Miss Manning whom she followed as headmistress in 1927. Both headteachers had won the respect of all who knew them for their devotion to young people and St Mary's Church.

One of Fr Bernard McIver's earliest memories of St Mary's – he was to recall with amusement 30 years later – was of arriving to join the staff at Bristol and on climbing the steps to the presbytery door being confronted by one of the Misses Turner towering above him at the head of a further small flight beyond.[1]

The Misses Turner, Mary and Nellie, had come to St Mary's from Clitheroe in Lancashire with Fr Robert Moss in 1907. In addition to housekeeping at the presbytery – where the day started at 6 a.m. – they had, in a variety of ways, served the church and parish with devotion over a period of 47 years. Fr Joseph Doyle enjoyed asking people if they knew anybody who had two mothers, and would then answer his own question by saying: "I have – Mary and Nellie."

The retirement of the two headteachers marked the occasion when St Mary's ceased to have secondary schools of its own, and pupils over 11 years of age went to the new St Thomas More School in Muller Road. The former secondary school buildings in Lower Park Row and Trenchard Street were adapted as more spacious premises for the use of St Mary's juniors and infants, a mixed school under Miss M.B. Kirby.

By 1956 a microphone had been installed in the pulpit and loudspeakers in the body of the church; the system was later extended to amplify the voices of the priests and choir from the sanctuary. There was no evening Mass on Sundays but there were four Masses in the morning – at 6.30, 8.00, 9.30, and 11.00. Not surprisingly the early morning services were not as popular as the Masses at 9.30 and 11 a.m. which were very well attended with the congregation filling the church, including the area of the

Sacred Heart chapel. There were protests that the dignity of the chapel was threatened by the press of worshippers and for a time the altar was roped off.

But the decline in the number of people with homes in the parish continued; it was estimated that 244 St Mary's families had left the district since 1954, leaving about 530 families still in residence.

On Sunday, September 15, 1957, a new set of Stations of the Cross was erected in the church by Fr Edgar Larway O.F.M., from St Bonaventure's Friary, and so was completed a project that was started by Miss Mary Caple after the redecoration of the church in the summer of 1951. It was five years in the finishing because a new heating system for the church and club rooms, costing thousands of pounds, had become a priority. Unable to find in the showrooms any set of Stations that would accord with the neo-classical architecture of St Mary's, Fr Crehan arranged for a firm of wood-carvers in northern Italy to make new Stations for £350; colour samples were sent over so that the painting of the set should match the existing decorative scheme in the church.

It was fitting that the Franciscans should be involved in the ceremony of installation. Their Order had been guardians of the Holy Places in the Middle Ages and it was through them that the practice of making the Way of the Cross spread from Palestine to all parts of Christendom.

The old Stations, which were a set of oil paintings bought from the artist in 1909 by Fr Robert Moss, were handed over to the Little Sisters of the Poor in Cotham.

Fr Lawrence Crehan, who had been almost 13 years at St Mary's, left in 1957 and later served at Edinburgh and Glasgow and in Rhodesia. A kindly, cheerful and sympathetic priest, he had a genuine love for St Mary's and its people and continued to keep in touch until his untimely death.

Fr Isaiah Capaldi, a devout, scholarly man, now took over the parish.

A popular broadcasting feature took place in St Mary's on Sunday, February 9, 1958. The B.B.C.'s weekly half-hour programme of Community Hymn Singing was broadcast from the church with a combined choir from the Catholic parishes of Bristol under the direction of St Mary's choir master, Frank

Duggan.

Another indication of St Mary's role as a city-centre Catholic church was the use made of it by outside Catholic organisations. The Catholic Civil Service Guild, the Catholic Deaf and Dumb Guild, the Catholic Corporation Employees, the Polish School, the Catholic Players, and the Italian Club were all users of St Mary's premises.

From time to time, well-known personalities from the world of entertainment performing in the theatres at the city centre are to be seen at St Mary-on-the-Quay. The church magazine for May 1958 reported the presence at a gathering of about 30 people in the parish hall of the distinguished actor, Peter O'Toole, who was playing *Hamlet* at the Bristol Old Vic. But his interest in the meeting was not explained – it had been called to discuss the formation of a football pool to aid parish funds!

It was about this time, in 1959, that the St Mary's committee added a 'new' social activity to their entertainment programme: "Do you Bingo?" they asked their fellow parishioners. "No, this is not the name of a modern dance nor a form of celebration, but a game that passes by the name of Housey-Housey and Tombola. It is being used as a money-raising scheme during the summer months. At the same time it provides a pleasant social evening for patrons." It was to be no passing fad – by the following year the church had already benefited to the extent of £500.

The decade ended for St Mary's with what amounted to a public letter of commendation from an unknown source. A letter to the *Bristol Evening Post* dated Saturday, December 12, 1959, and signed 'Caritas' was highlighted on the paper's religious affairs' page under the heading *Intrigued*:

> As a comparative stranger to Bristol, the church of St Mary's-on-the-Quay intrigues me. I attended Evening Mass last Tuesday, the Feast of the Immaculate Conception. The body of the church was full and overflowing into the gallery; sidesmen were 'making room'. Two-fifths were men, and about half the congregation received Holy Communion.
>
> There was no hymn-singing, no organ, no Bible reading, no sermon. The congregation of home-going city folk and

shoppers were certainly not wooed in any ordinary sense of the term. There had been a Mass that morning and another was to follow.

If a week-day feast is 'of obligation', such as Corpus Christi, the scene must be seen to be believed. On the last occasion I was wedged tightly into the gallery. I was fortunate, for there was an overflow into the street and approaching the altar rails was a major operation.

I have compared the above state of affairs with attendance at other city churches during, for instance, Holy Week, and found absolutely no comparison. What can be the reason?

Extensive renovation to the exterior of the church in the early sixties took about six months to complete. *The Somerset Countryman*, interesting itself in work being carried out on such a prominent building in the city, remarked: "The interior of this church was redecorated not long ago by the late Mr Goodhart-Rendel, but comparatively little was then done on the portico, and nothing at all on the rustication just above the pavement. These matters are all actively in hand, and St Mary-on-the-Quay will soon be an even better feature than before of the upper part of the Centre where this fine work by the Bristol architect R.S. Pope has long, by the dignity and good proportions of its neoclassicism, put some of its neighbours to shame."

One of the first tasks was to erect a new cross on top of the church as the iron clamp holding the old one had eaten away the stonework. Other work such as the building of new steps went according to plan, but the greatest challenge came not from the building itself but from pigeons and the damage and filth they caused. So persistent were they that to keep them outside the church the parish priest, Fr Capaldi, had to keep the windows shut, even in warm weather. The fight against the pigeon menace continued for some years and in 1964 the B.B.C. considered it of sufficient public interest to feature it on television. Another attempt to prevent the pigeons from making the church their haven met with some success when nets were stretched over the ledges and high up under the roof of the portico.

The organ fund never reached the sum hoped for, but Fr Capaldi made the courageous decision to build a new instrument nevertheless and ordered the work to be set in hand. Although the pipes were still sited in the organ loft in the north transept, the new all-electric console was positioned by the Lady Altar in the south transept. There were consequences: the pulpit, which would have obscured the organist's view, was removed to the other side of the sanctuary. Ironically this then placed it, for purposes of the liturgy, in the correct position, for previously it had been in a position normally only permitted in cathedrals.

In a lengthy article on the new organ at St Mary's in the June, 1961 issue of *Musical Opinion,* the writer spoke of the console as being "one of the most sumptuous I have seen, being of polished oak, with roll top cover, draw stops and pistons of solid ivory, reed stops lettered in red and flue stops in black ... A noble instrument worthy of the building in which it stands."

There were six priests at St Mary's at this time, their services always in demand either in the parish or as supply staff at other churches in the city area. But there was further indication of the decline in numbers of worshippers actually residing in the parish: Confirmations were no longer held regularly, but at intervals of two or three years. By the time of the Visitation of the Bishop in 1966, the number of candidates from the diminished parish of St Mary's was just 45.

On May 11, 1962 Marguerite Fedden, who came from one of Bristol's oldest families and was well known to the St Mary's congregation, died at the age of 83. She was a prolific writer of books of Catholic interest – novels, plays, recollections – and of works on local history. She was a regular and valued contributor to St Mary's magazine since the early days of publication and was a loyal friend to the church.[2]

Then, towards the end of the year, an event occurred in Rome that had been anticipated and prepared for over three years and was eventually to have a profound effect on the practices of the Catholic Church throughout the world.

In 1959 Pope John XXIII, seeing the Church's need to face the changes of the twentieth century and to modernise its attitudes and ideas, announced his decision to summon a Council to review the Church's laws, rules and practices. Prior to his departure for this momentous gathering of the Church's bishops, Bishop Rudderham spoke of it in a Pastoral Letter dated February 20, 1962:

> A General Council of the Church is never called except in time of some grave need. The Pope has stated clearly that unity amongst Christians is one of the chief matters to be considered at this Council – not, of course, the only matter, but one which he has close at heart.

Anticipating some of the worrying questions which the forthcoming debate must have prompted, the Bishop continued:

> It must be stated plainly that the teaching which the Church received from Christ Our Lord is altogether unchangeable … The Church's own laws and discipline, her ceremonial, even her customs, may well be changed and altered. She has already modified them altogether: she could never say that the Eucharist was anything but the true Body and Blood of Christ. She might allow a much wider exercise of jurisdiction to the rulers of the Church in different countries: she could never deny or abrogate the supreme authority of the Pope as Head of the Church and Vicar of Jesus Christ.

So after due preparation the Second Vatican Council opened in Rome on October 11, 1962; its deliberations were to continue for three years.

On the death of Pope John, the new Pope, Paul VI, presided over the continuing work of the Council and in 1964 travelled to India, so showing his respect for non-Christian religions, and then visited Israel where he met the Chief Patriarch of the Eastern Church, the first meeting of its kind for 1,000 years. Co-operation between Roman Catholics and other denominations, and between the Church and Laity, in which lay people were to become more involved with the day-to-day running of the Church, were some of the important outcomes of the Second Vatican Council, the final session of which was held in 1965, concluding with Mass in St Peter's Square.

Of Mary, the mother of Christ, Vatican II pronounced in

ringing tones: "[She] unites and re-echoes the greatest teachings of the faith ... [She is] the spotless image of all the Church desires and hopes wholly to be ... [She] shines towards the whole community of the elect as the model of all virtues." She is, Pope Paul declared, the Mother of the Church.

There were to be changes to the form of worship, the most significant being that the service was to be said in the language of the country instead of in Latin, the priest was to face the congregation at Mass, and the people were to be involved with the celebration: "Mother Church earnestly desires that all the faithful be led to that full, active and conscious participation in liturgical celebrations which is demanded by the very nature of the liturgy."

The first time English was used during the Mass at St Mary's was at the 6.30 a.m. service on the First Sunday of Advent, 1965, although it was not on that occasion said facing the people and was still partly in Latin. This was in the time when Fr Arthur Kavanagh was parish priest. Fr Capaldi had served St Mary's well, but his heart was in Scotland and he was glad to return there to take up a new appointment at Stornoway in the Western Isles. His departure marked a period during which he and two other priests, Fr J. Doyle and Fr L. Crehan, had served St Mary-on-the-Quay for a quarter of a century; all three revisited Bristol from time to time.

The new superior, Fr Kavanagh, came to St Mary's after considerable experience as parish priest at St George's, Worcester, and did much good work in Bristol. He rarely appeared in the limelight, but was a most effective hospital chaplain and a man of great charity.

By 1965 the daily Mass times had been established at 12.15 p.m. and 5.30 p.m., as they exist today; in addition there was also an 8 a.m. Mass attended by an average of 18 to 20 worshippers. On Sunday, May 22, 1966, a count taken in the church showed that 1,388 people attended the six Masses during the day.

Speaking of the Easter services in 1966, Fr Kavanagh remarked:

The Easter services went off very well in our church this year, and those who took part are thanked for combining so well. Most of the service was in English which in the shortened and rearranged version really made it much more appealing. Certainly more than the services of my youth when one had to listen to Twelve Lessons chanted in Latin, with quite lengthy and repetitious parts interspersed by the choir between lessons. It was an excellent penance, but of doubtful value for the enlightenment of the mind.

It was a time when St Mary's was well staffed with six priests, and it was possible for confessions to be heard in French, Spanish, German and Italian. The total number of altar servers was probably in the region of 30 or more – there might, for example, be as many as a dozen serving at the 9.30 a.m. Mass.

The 40-hour Exposition of the Blessed Sacrament (Quarant' Ore) which had long been celebrated in the diocese was usually held at St Mary's in January: it would begin with High Mass at 11 o'clock on Sunday and end on Tuesday morning with the Solemn Mass of Deposition. The Devotion of the 'Forty Hour' prayer, arranged in such a manner that, by one mission succeeding another, the Blessed Sacrament might be exposed to the veneration of the faithful in some church of the diocese every day during most of the year, began in Milan in the first half of the sixteenth century. Nearer our own time and in the Clifton Diocese, it was established by Bishop Clifford in 1868, and was first celebrated at St Mary's on March 15 of that year. A hundred years later, 99 churches in the diocese were taking part.[3]

There was a worrying decline in the number of pupils attending St Mary's Primary School in Lower Park Row. At the beginning of the decade, under the headship of Miss M.B. Kirby, there had been 219 on register, but by 1962 the number had fallen to 105 and the following year to 78. Although the numbers increased slightly for a while, it had become the smallest of the Catholic primary schools in the city. Miss Kirby was succeeded by Mr J. Quinn and, despite a surge in numbers to 133, it closed on July 16, 1971; Mr Quinn then became Headmaster of St Bernadette's Primary School and the former St Mary's pupils were accommodated elsewhere in the more modern premises of other, larger Catholic schools. It meant an end of the Wednesday morning 9 o'clock services at St Mary's which the boys and girls always attended before lessons – Mass followed by Benediction – and the familiar sight at the Sunday 9.30 Mass of the first half-dozen pews occupied by school children with their teacher. It heralded, too, the end of Sunday afternoon Catechism, regularly attended in the past by upwards of 200 young people.

Another enforced closure occurred in 1967 when the Sisters of the Convent of Mercy in Dighton Street, which had close connections with St Mary-on-the-Quay, were faced with considerable costs should they bring their school building up to the standard required. In addition, the movement of population to the outer suburbs had reduced the need for Catholic schools, such as theirs, in the centre of the city. The call for their services lay elsewhere and the Sisters left to join other convents of their Order at Westbury-on-Trym and Clevedon.

The Sisters of Mercy had first come to Bristol 121 years previously, when four Sisters of the Order from Bermondsey,[4] London, (who had been educated at the Franciscan convent at Taunton) arrived at Temple Meads Station on February 20, 1846 and, accompanied by Dr Brindle, went on to meet the Fathers at the presbytery in Trenchard Street. From there they were taken to their new home in Portland Square where furniture and beds were provided. Later, adapting a stable and coach house for the purpose, the Sisters opened the first free school for Catholic girls, but when as the numbers grew they were forced to seek larger premises they purchased at a cost of £3,000 Harwood House in Dighton Street where, on the feast of St Michael 1846, the Sisters went to live.

Very early during the Sisters' residence in Bristol, the Jesuit Fathers, who had returned to the city in 1847, were appointed their Spiritual Directors. The Sisters of Mercy continued to teach the children at St Joseph's as well as carrying out works of mercy in the city, visiting the sick and infirm and holding catechism classes. Later an orphanage for girls was opened.

In 1896 the Sisters celebrated the Golden Jubilee of the foundation of their convent in Dighton Street, an event that was marked by this tribute from the Catholics of Bristol:

It will indeed be a joy to you to realise that during the long space of fifty years you have, by the blessing of God, been

called to accomplish in your quiet and humble way such
great and good work to the poor and suffering of Bristol,
and to have so largely aided in the great cause of Christian
Education in this city ... You have visited the sick and the
dying among us, and greatly indeed did we value the
kindly, cheerful and generously given help and consolation
so much needed in those hours of trial and suffering ... We
thank God that he has given us such earnest, true, sincere
friends.[5]

In 1909 the Sisters from Dighton Street (they had established
another convent at Westbury-on-Trym) commenced teaching in
the Parish Senior School at St Mary-on-the-Quay; at this time
they were also teaching at an independent all-age school attached
to their convent, attended by many pupils from all areas of the
city. And in 1951 they started a hostel for young women.

The visiting they regularly engaged in had its lighter moments.
At one particular house in the parish, the Sisters were always
offered tea which, to their surprise, was made in a kettle instead
of a teapot. Thinking she was being helpful, one of the Sisters
gave the lady of the house a present of a teapot which, although
she received it without too much pleasure, she nevertheless used
on one or two subsequent visits. But old habits die hard and on
the third occasion the Sisters were surprised that once again they
were offered tea from the kettle. Where, then, was the teapot? It
had not been discarded: it now adorned the good lady's window-
sill – and from it grew a handsome geranium!

The Italian, Greek and Polish communities were amongst
many groups in the city who valued the work of the Sisters and
regretted their departure from the convent in Dighton Street.

Throughout the years, the Sisters of Mercy worked closely
with the Jesuits in Bristol, concerning themselves with the
spiritual welfare and social life of the parish. St Mary's had
special reason to be thankful to the Sisters for their contribution
to the work of the church and its schools. They will, indeed,
always be remembered for their service in the cause of Catholic
education in Bristol.

On the evening of Thursday, July 20, 1967, parishioners past
and present of St Mary's gathered at the convent's St Gabriel's

School to pay tribute to the Sisters and to take their leave. When the Sisters of Mercy left Dighton Street that year, Fr Arthur Kavanagh, the parish priest, was quick to praise the "many members of that religious community who have served our parish and our church so well and for so long." He described the closure of their convent as a bereavement for the city. But the good work of the Sisters of Mercy continues today through the presence of Sister Angela, as Parish Sister.

In the vicinity of Trenchard Street a big entertainment centre and multi-storey car park were in the process of being built and it seemed as though the presbytery itself would soon be under threat. The church, though, continued to serve the diverse requirements made on a city-centre church. St Patrick's Day in 1968, being a Sunday, could not be celebrated liturgically and an International Sunday was held instead: the Ukranians, the Hungarians, the Poles and the Italians each had Mass said by their own priests, or had at least a sermon from their own clergy. Fr Kavanagh reported a total of ten Masses said in St Mary's for the Catholics of Bristol that day.

When Fr Vincent Norbury took over in October 1968, he was appreciative of the generous and cooperative manner in which Fr Kavanagh introduced him to the parish and recognised the outstanding quality of kindliness he radiated in all he did. Fr Kavanagh left to be parish priest for the community at Tisbury in Wiltshire, the parish that serves the famous church of Wardour.[6]

NOTES

1. The presbytery entrance, with its disconcerting steps, was replaced in 1959 by another a few feet away at pavement level.
2. During the rectorship of Fr Joseph Doyle, Marguerite Fedden produced a small 18-page booklet entitled *Notes on the History of St Mary's-on-the-Quay*. It also deals with post-Reformation Catholicism in Bristol prior to 1843, leaving half a dozen pages devoted to St Mary's.

Two other writers who, after Marguerite Fedden, became regular and valued contributors to St Mary's magazine were Mary Friend and Kathleen Gallagher.

3. "The most common explanation for the choice of 40 is that it signifies the approximate number of hours that our Lord's body lay in the tomb between His death and His resurrection on the third day." *New Catholic Encyclopedia*, 1967.

4. Some 10 years later, nuns from the Bermondsey convent distinguished themselves as nurses working under Florence Nightingale in the Crimean War.

5. Extract from the Annals of the Sisters of Mercy, Dighton Street, Bristol.

6. "From the time of Elizabeth I to the suppression of the Society of Jesus in 1773, the Jesuits had been at Wardour, with the exception only of the years following the Oates Plot when several of their number had been executed and many more imprisoned ... Finally the [new] church was opened by Bishop Walmesley, the Vicar Apostolic of the western district, on the feast of All Saints 1776 with ecclesiastical ceremonial not seen by Catholics in England since the Reformation." *Wardour – A short history* by Philip Caraman, S.J., 1984.

A new St Mary-on-the-Quay. A model for a new St Mary's church, and office block behind, to be built on the existing site. This was one of the plans under consideration in the late 1960s and 70s. Note the pedestrian walkway above street level. See Chapter 15. (Photo: Jesuit Archives)

CHAPTER 15
Plans for a New Church

There are over 3,600 Listed Buildings in Bristol: St Mary-on-the-Quay is one of them. Such buildings being of architectural or historical importance, the City Council is required by Act of Parliament to ensure that all works on them are sensitive to their architectural character and history, and any work which alters the character of the building will need Listed Building Consent from the city authorities.

St Mary's was made a grade 2 listed building on January 8th, 1959. The entry in the Council's *List of Buildings of Special Architectural or Historic Interest* reads:

> 1839 R.S. Pope. 'Greek' portico of 6 Corinthian columns
> under a pediment. Inner porch has 2 columns 'in antis'.
> Plain wings with blocked architrave doorways. Base.
> Cruciform interior with wide nave: chancel is top lit and
> framed by 2 columns 'in antis'. Remains of galleries.

In the late 1960s, under Fr Vincent Norbury, St Mary's entertained ambitious plans for the re-development of its site in Colston Avenue. The new parish priest was thinking of a complete renovation of St Mary's so that the building could supply all the requirements of the liturgy and at the same time incorporate a presbytery to replace the existing building 200 yards distant in Trenchard Street. Prompted by the plans of developers to build an 18-storey office block with an elegant high-level walkway on one side of the church, and on the other side to develop Northcliffe House into a set of prestige office buildings, St Mary's was caught up in the spirit of the times: "Both [developments] will show up even more the shabbiness of this city church of ours and will make us sensitive even more to the question of what our contemporary church should be like. How do we see ourselves entering and competing in this nuclear age?

All this is extremely relevant to the scale as well as the urgency of getting on with this task."

Architects were engaged to draw up plans for the St Mary's site which would provide not only for a church with a white fibre-glass spire but also shops, offices and presbytery, with car-parking facilities at the rear. A front elevation sketch by Ivor Day and O'Brien of Queen Square in January 1969 shows an office block, wider though lower than the adjacent Colston office tower, and, rising in front of it as a canopy, an elegant curved spire indicating the presence of a church. The entrance is from a pedestrian walk-way above the shops at street level.

A model of this controversial scheme – radical, for the existing St Mary's building would be demolished – was put on display and became front page news in the *Bristol Evening Post* and the subject of comment on television; the Catholic newspaper *The Universe* featured it prominently in an almost page-length article. The city's Planning Committee deferred their decision on the project to allow time for public debate; in the meantime they referred the plans to the Royal Fine Arts Commission, who, particularly conscious that under the new proposals the neo-classical façade of the church would disappear, voiced their disapproval.[1] At this stage, March 1969, the Trustees of St Mary's, realising consent would not ultimately be given, withdrew the scheme from any further consideration by the Planning Authority. Although in the foreseeable future it is unlikely that St Mary's will be removed from the List, it is interesting to examine the other kinds of alterations that were being considered when proposals for change were sought.

In 1976 the architects, Broadbent, Hastings, Reid and New of Twickenham, Middlesex, put forward a number of schemes. One of them allowed for parking under the church for 16 cars, with an entrance and separate exit on Colston Avenue. Since this would occupy the existing hall area, a new space for social activities was to be created where the body of the church now is. The nave and sanctuary would then be situated on a new floor built at a height of 23 feet – over 12 feet above the existing church floor level.

Within the same scheme, another radical plan placed the Blessed Sacrament Chapel, with 30 seats, beyond the High Altar, and the Priests' Sacristy beyond that again.

Other plans likewise proposed the building of new floors. In every case the façade of the church was retained, but the architects redesigned the area to the rear of the church, fronting Host Street, in various ways; one scheme provided for a kitchen, cloakroom and lavatories, and parking space for five cars.

In some schemes there was provision for a lift. To avoid having to climb stairs? The architects had a wider vision:

> The lift, while serving all floors, can also be used by
> disabled parishioners to get from Host Street level to
> Church and Hall below. Also it can be used for funerals, it
> being an easy operation to lower a coffin to Sanctuary level
> and raise afterwards to the waiting hearse in the car park
> above.

The boon of a car park was to be denied St Mary's. The Highway Authority, viewing things from a different stance and deciding this was a case of one man's meat being another man's poison, saw the scheme for underground parking as adding to the existing problems caused by traffic swirling round the city centre – and vetoed it. Nor would they countenance access into the site from Host Street, at the rear, except for those living in the buildings.

It seemed to the architects that the best course to follow would be to retain the main church buildings but demolish all the outbuildings around the site and replan the accommodation within that shell as far as possible. The basic decisions to be made, they felt, should answer the following questions: Is the church to be placed at ground level in Colston Avenue with the main hall placed at Host Street level, or should the hall be placed at Colston Avenue level and the church 23 feet above at the level of Host Street in the rear?

As for the future of all these plans, the architects stated the position in a letter to Bishop Alexander at the end of 1977: "Application for Planning Consent is held over by the Planning Authority until a decision regarding the future of the Trenchard Street site is reached."

In the event the cost of the works (£320,000 for the final

scheme) proved prohibitive, even with the proceeds from the sale of the Trenchard Street site, and the plans languish in the archives forsaken or to await their hour.

NOTES

1. "The façades of listed buildings are often a complete composition and should be carefully conserved."

"Alterations such as changes of internal layout, erection or removal of internal partitions or the removal of period features will be resisted." *Bristol City Centre Draft Local Plan, City Centre Policy Schedule*, April 1992, p.18.

CHAPTER 16
St Mary's Magazine –
and a New Cathedral

The idea of starting a parish magazine had first been broached at a meeting in 1951[1] of the Entertainments Committee (the parish committee of its day). Fr Lawrence Crehan was attending for the first time as parish priest and the magazine – which was to endure and be such a success – was his brain-child. Philip Golden, a convert to Catholicism at the outbreak of war in which he served in the Royal Navy, offered to be editor and Marian Savidge became secretary. It was a working partnership that lasted over twenty-five years during which a well-organised, thoughtful, informative and entertaining magazine was produced monthly, and has continued to this day. So a new dimension was added to parish life, a means whereby the sick and housebound and those living afar, Catholic and non-Catholic, could be linked to worship, people and events at St Mary-on-the-Quay.

The first important anniversary of the magazine was with the appearance of the 250th issue in October 1972. It was acknowledged by Bishop Joseph Rudderham: "In its pages will be a record of the life and activity that has gone on amongst you these 21 years: much has now attained the status of history – and the sort of history which really shows the life and work which has been achieved over the years. But it is a living history, and may it continue for many years to come."

The parish priest at the time, Fr Vincent Norbury, remarked that already there were 20 bound volumes of St Mary's magazine on the editor's shelves "in which the trivial jostle side by side with some outstanding parochial event. The first evening Mass (Ascension '53), Ignatian Year (1956), Marian Year (1958), a Bishop's Visitation. Our memories may fade. Our interest in the past may fail before the relentless pressure of the present. No matter. There between the covers of these volumes the history of the parish is ever available. The Magazine is always ready to serve the parish which called it into being."

Four years later the printing on the handsome pale blue cover of the magazine for December proclaimed it to be the Silver Jubilee Number, 1951-1976; the number of pages had been increased from the usual 16 to 20, and to meet the cost of producing a special edition the editor had reluctantly raised the price to 6p. Bishop Alexander recognised the difficulty, not so much in producing a magazine, though this requires much work, but in maintaining it over many years after the novelty has worn off: "St Mary-on-the-Quay has benefited greatly from the wide range of its contributors. The Jesuit Fathers have written many valuable articles on a wide variety of subjects and this has been a great strength to the magazine over the years. Many parishioners have contributed reports, comments or letters and in this way the magazine managed to preserve a certain freshness and topicality in spite of its respectable age ... If all continue to play their part, there is no reason why the magazine should ever come to an end."

"It seems an age ago," recalled Marian Savidge, "when he [Fr Crehan] asked me at, of all places, a bus stop in Cotham Road, if I would like to 'do a bit of typing' – I said 'yes' without giving it much thought at the time as I was concentrating on the arrival of my bus. But that was my introduction to the magazine and the start of a long and pleasant partnership with our Editor, Phil.

"We've had minor panics over the years – One evening I remember arriving at the Presbytery [in Trenchard Street] and after looking for the key in its usual place, couldn't find it and at last discovered it had been locked in the office. Fortunately the window was open a little at the top and one of the priests (I believe it was Fr McIver) gallantly squeezed through the gap and rescued the key from inside."

Trawling for items from the magazines of 1952 to reprint for the jubilee year, Philip Golden came across the report of the Youth Club outing to Bournemouth: "After tea Fr L. Crehan visited the Sacred Heart Church and was much impressed by the amplification system in the pulpit and sanctuary, sufficiently so to plan one for St Mary's when funds allow."

The following piece had a tragic aftermath : "After a short

stay at St Mary-on-the-Quay Fr. Gerald Cooney S.J. sailed from Southampton on August 22nd to join the foreign Missions in British Guyana where he will join Fr Dinley who was so helpful to us when this Magazine was first mooted. Fr Cooney is an old boy of St Mary's where he will be remembered for his expert piano playing which was a feature of contemporary concerts." Sadly, four years after reprinting this, Philip Golden was reporting Gerald Cooney's murder in Guyana, a country to which he had given such dedicated service.

And because a well-balanced magazine finds room for the trivial as well as the serious, the July issue for 1952 reported: "The winner of the £1 prize for the balloon race, organised in connection with the Garden Fete at Nazareth House, was Cecilia McCarthy of 54 Kingsdown Parade. Her balloon reached Exeter." Tongue-in-cheek, the editor had penned a suitable heading: "Another Success for St Mary's," he announced with satisfaction.

On February 1, 1977, Bishop Alexander presented Philip Golden and Marian Savidge with the papal award Bene Merenti. They continued their working partnership until both retired in 1985. Philip Golden had been editor for 34 years. The parish priest estimated that Marian Savidge had already typed over 800,000 words for the magazine – but he was speaking at the beginning of 1955 when the magazine was only four years old![2]

On April 25, 1972, over 20 bishops attended the consecration of Dr Mervyn Alexander as Auxiliary Bishop of the Diocese of Clifton. Also present at the impressive ceremony at the Pro-Cathedral in Bristol were five Anglican bishops, over 100 priests and an even greater number of nuns. "Homeliness, simplicity, warmth, community, oneness, especially with the newly-ordained Bishop – these were distinctive and impressive features of this memorable occasion." So the parish priest of St Mary's recalled the event, in offering the congratulations of his congregation.

Bishop Alexander's first visit to St Mary's was on July 31, to celebrate the Feast of St Ignatius, a visit he has repeated many times since. His crozier was the one used by Bishop Hendren, who in 1848 was consecrated Vicar-Apostolic of the Western

District at St Mary-on-the-Quay, and became, on the Restoration
of the Hierarchy, the first Bishop of Clifton.

The consecration of Bishop Alexander was the last big event
at the Pro-Cathedral before its closure and the opening in June
1973 of the new Cathedral Church of SS Peter and Paul a short
distance away. Any doubts some people entertained about the
startingly unconventional architecture of the new building in
Pembroke Road found no place in the wholehearted acclaim
given it by the parish priest of St Mary's:

> I was able to inspect the Cathedral whilst the finishing
> touches were put to it, and I can only record an impression
> of satisfaction and delight. Here was a pocket Cathedral,
> compact, lofty, inspiring awe and reverence. Here was
> mystery expressed so subtly in the various depths and levels
> and angles of ceiling, and in the irregularity of contours.
> The building held many surprises: the unexpected was
> always appearing. Art and craftsmanship provided at
> different twists and turns so many sources of satisfaction. It
> will be a long time before we appreciate to the full the
> richness of the design both within and without. This could
> well be esteemed as cathedral architecture at its very best.
> And an age might well be proud to end its career on this
> sublime architectural triumph.[3]

Fr Norbury's congregation had raised money to make a
contribution of their own: the young Madonna structured in
bronze by Terry Jones was a gift from St Mary's parish. A
nation-wide audience had the chance to see it when the B.B.C.
televised *Songs of Praise* from the Cathedral on Sunday 16, 1984.

Of course, said Philip Golden, editor of St Mary's magazine,
the new cathedral had its critics, but he described them as being
of a "mild variety". There was one aspect of the architect's work,
however, that "baffled" him: When sitting or kneeling the
worshipper had an uninterrupted view of the altar, but when he
stood his view was obstructed by a taller person in front. To this
personal observation he added what he considered "the one main
general criticism" – it concerned the Stations of the Cross:
"Certainly the Stations have been the only part of the splendid

cathedral that have aroused any real passion."

The Cathedral was consecrated on June 29, 1973 by Bishop Joseph Rudderham and the address given by Cardinal Heenan; a few weeks later it was visited by Her Majesty, Queen Elizabeth II. Catholics in the diocese had, said the Bishop, "at last a worthy Cathedral, purpose-built for the new rite in which the Holy Sacrifice of the Mass is celebrated."

On August 31, 1974 Bishop Rudderham retired and on March 5, 1975 Bishop Alexander was installed in Clifton Cathdral as the eighth Bishop of the Diocese.

NOTES

1. 1951 also saw the first issue of the *Clifton Diocesan Directory*.
2. There are bound volumes of the Magazine covering almost four decades.
3. *St Mary-on-the-Quay Magazine*, July, 1973.

The largest of the three pictures by Italian artists of the mid-nineteenth century which span the wall above the gallery at the back of the church. (Photo: Bill Joll)

CHAPTER 17

Important Changes at St Mary's

Fr Henry Waterhouse had just switched on the television at the Trenchard Street presbytery one evening in May 1974 when, the parish priest being away, he was summoned to answer a telephone call from a man who lived some miles distant but was anxious to talk to a priest from St Mary's. The purpose of his call was, initially, something of a puzzle. A long quotation read from a Catholic periodical was followed by half an hour of complaints: the man's place was then taken by his wife who had asked to speak. By now their arguments had taken shape: they were objecting to recent changes in the Church.

Like other parishes St Mary's was earnestly engaged on implementing the decrees of the Second Vatican Council. Consultation and explanation there had been in plenty, though clearly never enough for those who will always prefer the old ways and find it truly hard to change. Yet over the centuries there have been many changes in the ceremonies of the Mass and the practice of Holy Communion, and the Mass as it was at the time of the Second Vatican Council had existed for less than four centuries.

The Liturgical Group, made up of clergy and laity with various viewpoints, was one of at least 12 committees at St Mary's in 1972 considering different aspects of parish life. The Group saw the Masses (there were six on a Sunday) as capable of different emphases: the devotional Mass, the family Mass, the Solemn Mass, the Sunday afternoon Mass and the Folk Mass. Varied, complementary, valid – appealing, it was hoped, to different congregations.

A Folk Mass was held monthly on the First Friday at 8 p.m. in the crypt of St Mary's and was the responsibility of the Central Catholic Club, a lively and successful social group of young people between the ages of 18 and 30, who welcomed also Catholics from other parishes, and non-Catholics too. The club was started by Fr F. Lobo and the Legion of Mary, and the Sunday evening meetings were very popular. "This Mass is always very unusual!" the club boldly declared, but were at pains to allay suspicions and to explain the use of guitars, recorders and other kinds of musical accompaniment; the Constitution of the Sacred Liturgy, Vatican II, they said, countenanced the introduction of other instruments for use in divine worship.

The Folk Mass, a regular event, was often taken by visiting priests, including Bishop Alexander who on occasions joined young people from St Mary's and other churches in walks organised by the Bristol Youth Service Council, along the wooded trails of the Forest of Dean, and in the evening celebrated a Folk Mass in the open air. "Episcotreks" St Mary's magazine liked to call them. For a while a Folk Mass was held on Sundays. All of which prompted Fr Kenneth Nugent, when he left St Mary's for the Catholic chaplaincy at Keele University, to write: "Keele still benefits from my invaluable apprenticeship in Bristol. House Masses, Folk Masses and ecumenical happenings are all part of the routine now ... All I need now is a crypt!"

The practice of members of the congregation exchanging the Sign of Peace was recommended by the Bishops' Conference at Easter 1972 and was first introduced at St Mary's, most appropriately, at the Midnight Mass in December; the congregation was then invited to join in giving one another the Sign of Peace at every Mass in future. The Sign, which comes before Holy Communion, has occupied this position in the Latin Rite for some 14 centuries.

It was only from 1970 that use was made of lay readers at St Mary's; then, following the Hierarchy's Low Week meeting on May 3, 1973, the following simple statement was issued by the Catholic Information Office, further evidence of the Church's new thinking on the important role that women play in Church life: "Women may now read the Word of God during Mass from the same place as men readers." The explanatory note Fr Vincent Norbury, parish priest, issued by way of introducing the new practice to St Mary's carries today, perhaps inevitably, overtones that were never intended, but he was then treading new ground and proceeding with caution:

Formerly no female was allowed on the sanctuary during a service. The sanctuary was divided and shut off from the congregation and only priests and male servers were allowed to serve there. But to-day the new liturgy wants the altar to be close to the faithful and the sanctuary open to participation ... And this participation is for all parties, apart from the sacred ministers, men and women, boys and girls and choir.

It is natural for the older generation to wince at the sight of a woman at the high point in the service ascending the sanctuary steps and occupying the pulpit. Old changes die slowly and liturgical tastes are as hard to change as our personal tastes in food. Which only emphasises the problem of respecting the Old while remaining open to the New.

In the light of this I first of all suggest we should be open to the principle of women readers on Sundays and weekdays at all Masses; that where we have older boys reading, there should also be an opportunity for older girls to read: that where we have established rotas of male readers there should be introduced a modicum of female readers: that at Masses where we can find no male reader we shall be prepared to invite a female reader, if one is available: that all readers, male or female, should be properly trained for this official function of the Liturgy.[1]

So, the green light had been given and St Mary's was making a modest start. It was a difficult period for those who had to implement the changes of Vatican II: discernment, determination and tact were qualities invariably needed.

One more important Liturgical change occurred a year later. In the twelfth and thirteenth centuries a bitter controversy had raged concerning Communion under both kinds: if only the species of bread was given, was the communicant truly receiving Christ's Body and Blood in the sacrament? To clarify the position Rome decreed in 1415, and again in 1562 at the Council of Trent, that a communicant could truly receive under only one kind. Then in 1962, although upholding the dogmatic principles laid down by the Council of Trent, Vatican II said: "Communion under both kinds may be granted when Bishops think fit, not only to clerics and religious, but also to the laity." So the Church gradually returned to what had been its practice during the first thousand years of its history, and in March of 1974 Bishop Rudderham wrote: "On the recommendation of the Liturgy Commission and the Council of Priests, I authorize the administration of Holy Communion under both kinds at weekday Masses, whenever the Parish Priest is convinced the people have been prepared for it and desire it." Communion under both kinds commenced at St Mary's on Monday, June 3, and from then on was given at all weekday Masses, with the majority of worshippers participating.

The Roman Church, post Vatican II, was outward-looking in a new sense – Catholics were urged to be ecumenically minded and to find ways in which this might find practical expression in the cause of Christian unity. To this end the Catholic Truth Society, back in 1968, had produced a booklet entitled *Ecumenical Directory*, with the sub-title: "Directory for the application of the decisions of the Second Ecumenical Council of the Vatican concerning Ecumenical Matters".

An interesting venture in ecumenism occurred in September 1969 when Canon A.B.Webster, Warden of the Anglican Lincoln Theological College, and eight of his students visited St Mary's for a week to share in the life of a Catholic parish. The students were accommodated in the homes of members of the congregation, attended services at St Mary's as well as at Anglican churches, experienced various aspects of parish work, visited Catholic schools, and enjoyed opportunities for discussion with prominent people in the city. Reflecting on the visit their leader observed: "Our group was overwhelmed by the kindness and openness with which we were received and accepted ... The abiding impressions of our stay are of hope, not despair; of love, not fear. I do not think that any of us in the future will so easily fall into the trap of regarding the boundaries of the Church as including just the members of our own particular denomination."

St Mary's had an Ecumenical Group which met regularly (fortnightly at one time) and worked zealously to forge links with the city-centre churches, efforts which were reciprocated by the other denominations. But the Group early on recognised problems: "Not over-much progress has been made generally in getting people to become ecumenically minded."

It was naturally hoped that the South West Ecumenical Congress to be held in Bristol in 1973 would arouse great interest, and certainly amongst the congregation of St Mary's in whose parish boundaries many of the activities planned would take place. The Congress (there were to be others) which had been prepared over 18 months by many ecumenical groups, including St Mary's, began with a Unity Service in Bristol Cathedral on Friday evening, April 6, in which the Bishops of Bristol and Clifton took part; Saturday was devoted to Section Conferences at eight centres throughout the city, and on the Sunday morning the B.B.C. televised the Congress Service held in a Baptist church. The climax was the gathering of 2,000 people in the Colston Hall on Sunday afternoon when the Archbishop of Canterbury and Cardinal Suenens spoke on their "Vision of the Future of the Christian Church". Another South West Ecumenical Congress was held three years later.

Ecumenism has made for a new openness amongst the Churches, and an appreciation of the richness to be found in the many facets of world-wide Christianity, but it is clearly difficult for many of the faithful, of whatever denomination, to feel their practical energies engaged in what seems a peripheral activity when they are so committed to their own Church. They fear loss of identity. The ideal of Christian Unity they embrace whole-heartedly: Ecumenism they recognise readily – perhaps with a friendly nod in passing by. Fr Tom Connor, parish priest at a later date, restated the obligations of St Mary's congregation in this field: "It is often said that the lack of unity among Christians is one of the greatest obstacles to the spread of Christianity. Within the laws and guidelines of the Church we must all be ecumenists and strive to remove the obstacle." Indeed, on the occasion of Pope John Paul II's momentous visit to Ireland in 1979 (a few of the St Mary's congregation made the journey to Phoenix Park, Dublin, or to Knock) he appealed for "Common Witness".

Five years after the church began implementing some of the changes recommended by the Bishops at the Second Vatican Council the parish annual general meeting of 1975 was given reports on the progress that had been made. While acknowledging the hard work that had been continuing with the groups, it was hoped to revitalise some of them, including the one concerning itself with ecumenical matters. It was felt that the Ecumenical Group was functioning satisfactorily despite considerable apathy, which prompted Fr Vincent Norbury to stress that "in face of unbridled secularism it was more and more necessary for churches to unite." Despite the apathy of many people, by the 1980s the Ecumenical Group at St Mary's was the lone survivor of the church's Pastoral Renewal Groups of the early seventies.

Amidst these radical changes the life of the parish continued. It was in Fr Norbury's time that a mixed choir was started under James Proctor, but after a short while Victor Venning was appointed choirmaster and remained in charge until his death in 1987.

In February, 1970, Fr Vincent Norbury travelled to London to join other Jesuits in a meeting with the Father General of the Society of Jesus, Pedro Arrupe.[2] This was only the third visit of a General to the English Province since the Society was formed in the sixteenth century. On this historic occasion he spoke with serenity and quiet confidence on aspects of the work and organisation of the Society, particularly in the context of the recent Vatican Council.

A welcome visitor to St Mary's in November was Fr Terence Corrigan who, the previous month, had just completed his term as Provincial of the English Province. Fr Corrigan, a Bristol man, had been ordained in St Mary's 25 years previously.

The ordination of Alan Fudge at St Mary's on Saturday, July 10, 1971, was an event eagerly awaited. Alan had been an altar server at St Mary's in the sixties, and later sacristan, and then accepting the vocational call he duly came under the authority of the Westminster diocese. Many guests travelled from London for the ordination ceremony, which was performed by Bishop Guazzelli, Auxiliary Bishop of Westminster. Present with the Bishop was the Rt Rev Mgr Thomas Hughes V.G. and among the concelebrants was Fr Alan's former parish priest and friend, Fr Isaiah Capaldi, revisiting after eight years.

Changes in the Eucharistic worship of the Church made it necessary for the Church to change its regulations about the ministers of Communion.

From its earliest days, for almost nine centuries, it had been the practice of the Church to reserve the Sacrament, and for deacons and lay people to take Communion from the church to the homes of the sick that they might thereby share in the Mass that had been celebrated; now, in the new Rite of Anointing and Pastoral Care of the Sick, priests were urged to ensure that the sick could receive Communion often and even daily during the Easter season.

There was another factor. The number of people coming forward to receive Communion, particularly under both kinds, could be so great that the priest would require help if the distribution was to be carried out in a reverent way and to avoid any suggestion of rushing. In his Instruction *Immensae Caritatis*, Pope Paul VI gave bishops the opportunity to designate lay men and women and religious brothers and sisters as Special, Auxiliary, or Extraordinary Ministers of Communion.

It was recommended that parishes should present a number of candidates for designation – mature Christians, of good character who, by their Christian living showed they took their Faith seriously – and if approved by the Bishop they would be sent on a course of formation by the Commission for the Liturgy and, in addition, attend a Day of Recollection. After this the Service of Commissioning would take place at the Cathedral.

On Whit Sunday June 6, 1976, Vincent Dimambro and Peter Caple became the first members of St Mary's congregation to be so commissioned at Clifton Cathedral and received their document of appointment:

MERVYN
BISHOP of CLIFTON

In virtue of the faculties granted by his Holiness Pope Paul VI in the Instruction of the Sacred Congregation for the Discipline of the Sacraments *Immensae Caritatis*, 29th January, 1973, I hereby appoint you as Extraordinary Minister of Holy Communion. This ministry may be exercised in the Diocese of Clifton in accordance with Diocesan Regulations.

Given at St Ambrose, Leigh Woods, this 6th day of June, 1976.

+ Mervyn Alexander
Bishop of Clifton

This was also the Sunday on which the option of receiving Communion in the hand was first observed at St Mary's.

The parish had changed. Chilcott's map of 1838[3] has the Irvingites' Church in position on Under the Bank, though their building, which was to become St Mary-on-the-Quay, had not then been completed. Host Street is boldly marked, as is Trenchard Street, though both are now little more than lanes in the context of city development. Look for the Colston Hall and we find, instead, Colston's School; and the Fathers walking from the presbytery to the end of their road would have reached not Colston Street, but a narrow cobbled road known as Steep Street. From this area it would have been possible to walk in any direction through streets lined with shops and houses.

The change has, of course, been continual, and the reasons for it many, but the result has been a decline over the years in the numbers of St Mary's congregation living in the parish. The old Catholic population in the Trenchard Street area has gone with the building of the Council House and the Entertainment Centre and car parks. So, too, have parishioners removed from the St James's district as a result of developments around Marlborough Street and beyond. St James's Back (now disappeared in its old form, where John Scudamore set up the first Catholic chapel), the Pithay leading off it, and Montague Street where the Jesuits had a house,[4] were all once part of a thickly populated area. The houses of Queen Square are no longer used as homes, nor are the buildings in King Street – but some of St Mary's congregation lived there once. To the north, hospital and university have, in part, created a new landscape.

There was a time when 2,000 people lived in that part of the parish around the presbytery, and there were pockets of Catholic population in other areas within walking distance of St Mary-on-the-Quay. Well-attended services, a busy social club, whist drives and dances, attested to a city-centre church that was the focus of Catholic life.

The Second World War was the biggest catalyst for change in the city, but even before then housing estates were being established on the outskirts, populated by former inner-city dwellers. The first housing estate was developed at Fishponds in 1920, at a time when a three-bedroomed house cost around a £1,000: a decade later the price had dropped to £400. By 1939 15,000 new dwellings had been erected, including estates at Sea Mills, Shirehampton, Horfield, Knowle and Bedminster; by the end of 1972, 33,461 council houses had been built post-war. New churches had to be built in these communities, and in establishing the new Catholic parishes, St Mary's families who had left their city homes played an important part.

We have seen how the grandiose schemes of the 1960s for redesigning St Mary's came to nothing. The strategy of the property developers to buy the Trenchard Street site, so providing the finance for the redesigning of St Mary's within a grand commercial development of the Colston Avenue site, was thwarted by the city Planning Authority, who after nearly three years' consideration rejected the plans. The dream of a new St Mary's, behind floodlit portico and incorporating a presbytery on the site, had faded.

But amidst the concern for their own church's future St Mary's parishioners voluntarily entered into a commitment to build a mission church overseas in, as it was then known, Rhodesia. It was a response to the Jesuit Missions' Rural Churches Campaign and intended to commemorate Holy Year in 1975. The initiative came from the Ladies Group of St Mary's, who launched a fund to raise £600. In the event, within a year this energetic group had raised £1,000 and building work started on August 26, 1975. The church, situated in Chiveso, was fittingly called "St Mary's".

By April 1976 the property boom and thus the optimum time for selling the Trenchard Street site for office development had passed, and while the developers were still awaiting the public enquiry which they had asked for some eight months previously to determine what could or could not be built there, St Mary's resigned itself to coping with their building problems from their own resources. "After some cosmetic surgery to halls and schools, the water is still pouring in, the fuel bills soar and we are not progressing at all," said Fr Norbury. "Just what is needed? ... Ambitious speculative schemes can no longer be considered in the light of planning restrictions and building costs. Building must be strictly geared to need. A modest workable scheme must be devised quickly ... on the existing St Mary's site and behind the classic portico.Could this not be a scheme for the future with a respect for the past? A museum? On the contrary, it could be the hub of Christian witness in the 21st century."

After eight and a half years at St Mary's, Fr Norbury was seconded for work on Retreats and was subsequently appointed to the well-known Jesuit church of St Aloysius in Glasgow. A man of wide-ranging interests and enthusiasms, generous, strong-willed yet tolerant, he experienced many disappointments over his ambitious plans for the development of St Mary's, which he had striven for from within months of his arrival in the parish, but in a delightful farewell to his congregation he confessed that for him the focal point of St Mary's was not the church, nor the middle hall, nor even the social club, but the presbytery:

> Many people seemed to climb those steps (one and one and eight) each day, or descend from the top yard to call on the presbytery, of all ranks and professions and trades and many too, at mid-day, who were of no fixed abode, and though the majority came at appointed times how often many came out of due time and were prepared to wait in dining rooms and passage ways and offices across the way. The presbytery was an open house and the congregation shared the presbytery only just a little less than the community. And for this I look back with great gratitude and joy that this was so ...
>
> I wouldn't want it moved an inch from this busy little side street which runs back into the centre of things and into history. In replanning St Mary's there has always been thought of building a presbytery beside the church, but no architect could ever redesign the atmosphere of No. 21 or reconstruct the memories, the pastoral care, the human tears and joys, the very stuff of all that's deepest and truest in the

human make-up, that made the meaning of the presbytery for me so rich – an antechamber to what the Lord Himself spoke so movingly about – His Father's House.[5]

Not want it moved an inch? His successor, Fr Thomas Connor, had other ideas.

NOTES

1. *St Mary-on-the-Quay Magazine*, December, 1973.
2. Fr Pedro Arrupe, the 28th Superior General of the Society of Jesus, died in 1991 at the age of 83. He led the Jesuits through a period of severe upheaval and a series of battles with the Papal Curia. He was the first Basque leader of the Jesuits since St Ignatius, the founder of their Society. Arrupe suffered a severe stroke in 1981 and the Pope installed his personal delegate, Fr Paolo Dezza, to govern the Society in his place. When Pope John Paul II allowed the Jesuits to select a successor to Arrupe in 1983, they chose Fr Pater-Hans Kolvenbach, a Dutchman.
3. Chilcott's map lists 26 "Churches"; 7 "Methodist Chapels"'; 10 "Independent Chapels"; 8 "Baptist Chapels"; 11 "Miscellaneous Chapels" (including St Joseph's). *A New Plan of Bristol, Clifton and the Hotwells* by J. Chilcott, 1838.
4. Fr Scudamore lived at No.29 Montague Street. *Sketchley's Directory* of 1775, the first Bristol Directory, has the following entry against this address: "Skudamore, Rev. John, R.-priest." His neigbours were Benjamin Thomas, book-keeper, and Ann Axford, widow. The Jesuit Archives in London show that in the last decade of the century the house was no longer needed by the Society and was let at a rent of £16 annually. It proved a troublesome property and was sold two years before the opening of St Mary's for £150.
5. *St Mary-on-the-Quay Magazine*, May, 1977.

The Lady Chapel, with the statues of St Joseph and St Ignatius Loyola, the founder of the Society of Jesus. (Photo: Bill Joll)

CHAPTER 18

St Mary's in Crisis

On his arrival, Fr Connor appraised the situation at St Mary-on-the-Quay with the sharp eye of a newcomer. He appreciated the warmth of the welcome he received, but as a stranger and, moreover, as one who had been required to uproot himself after ten and a half years in his previous appointment, he had no sentimental attachments to colour his perceptions: the presbytery was too far away from the church, which was therefore unattended for long periods each day; strangers had difficulty finding the presbytery and there was just one reception room for visitors; the disadvantages during inclement weather of two separate sites were obvious. Within the church, even with the temporary altar, the priest felt remote and far away from the people, and the communion rails were a hindrance. The halls were drab and very unsafe, and the church, considering the comparatively small numbers attending the services, costly to heat.

Under the circumstances it was not simply a routine visit that the English Provincial of the Society, Fr William Maher, paid to St Mary's in November 1977, seven months after Fr Connor's arrival. He strongly recommended that the number of Masses (seven, including the Saturday Mass carrying the Sunday obligation which had started at St Mary's on April 16) be reduced, and insisted that something be done very quickly about the church and presbytery. In the past, plan after plan had been rejected for one reason or another, but because some major development always seemed to be in the offing, maintenance work had been repeatedly postponed until some parts of church and presbytery were actually in danger of falling down. A meeting between Bishop Alexander, Father Provincial and the priests of St Mary's was to be arranged as soon as possible to decide on the best course of action. So the year ended with the future of St Mary's in question.

In the new year the congregation was given the opportunity to vote for the retention of five of the seven Masses for Sunday, and as a result the Masses at 12.15 p.m. and 7.45 p.m. were discontinued. The meeting between Bishop Alexander, Fr Provincial, priests and parishioners eventually took place at 8 p.m. on Monday, April 24th.

Neither Bishop Alexander nor Fr Connor sounded hopeful of St Mary's being able to raise the £300,000 necessary to renovate the buildings, a formidable sum for a church with net assets at that moment of £17,145. And to what extent should parishioners in future years be saddled with debt? Fr Connor (another doubting Thomas? he asked himself) nevertheless acknowledged that it was the wish of most of those present that they should try to save St Mary's despite the cost and he, with the Provincial's approval, determined to do his utmost to find the money. The following morning, as if to show that all would yet be well, he received a cheque for £500 from a lady who had been at the night's meeting. What he did not then know was that the Diocesan Finance Committee, about to launch a fund-raising campaign of its own throughout the city and diocese, felt unable to support St Mary's own appeal; and, as though heaping Ossa upon Pelion, the church's architect then made it clear that £300,000 would not be enough after all, as it took no account of value added tax, did not allow for annual inflation, and did not include professional fees. With unwitting irony the parish magazine that month carried some historical notes entitled: "How We Became St Mary-on-the-Quay". In the meantime rows of jugs, vases and buckets remained in place – catching drips from the leaking roofs.

How were the Jesuits to get the best price for the Trenchard Street property? Fr Henry Waterhouse explained to the congregation that the Trustees for the Society of Jesus, working from Farm Street in London, had retained the services of experienced estate agents to advise them, but various plans had been rejected by the Bristol authorities and one after another buildings on the site had been listed as being of historical or architectural interest and worthy of preservation. Now the City Council had changed its policy about office development and were interested in using the site for housing.

"Given the present state of affairs in the property market," said Fr Waterhouse, "it would seem a vain hope to find a private developer who would be ready to acquire the Trenchard Street site for housing. What sort of housing would give him a return on his investment? The only sensible solution that offered itself was to find a reputable housing association with the experience and resources needed for dealing with such a site. So the Trust's agents got busy immediately seeking one out and negotiations to sell have already begun."

A housing association acquiring its capital from public funds is assured of ready co-operation from the city planners and can count on getting 'listed building consent' to demolish buildings which would spoil the development. As for the price to be paid for a site involving a housing association, it is for the District Valuer to determine. "So if, by your prayers you can influence the mind of the District Valuer to fix a price that will be fair to us," Fr Waterhouse told one anxious parishioner, "you will put us all in your debt." So negotiations between the Society and a housing association proceeded. After the hopes, expectations and excitement of the palmy days, the drift towards anti-climax continued.

With the proposal by the Anglican authorities in Bristol to declare five of their local churches redundant, the St Mary's congregation considered a new solution to their troubled affairs – the possibility of using one of the vacated buildings if Bishop Tinsley's plans went through, instead of reordering their own church. Two nearby churches in particular commended themselves for St Mary's purposes, if available – St James and Christ Church. But over all was an air of unreality as nothing of significance materialised, and 1978 drew to a close.

By May 1979 a new costing had raised the total required by £51,500 to £351,500, increasing at one per cent a month. Should we even try to raise that amount of money for so few parishioners? asked Fr Connor. He was referring to the average Sunday Mass attendance at St Mary's which had shown a steady decline since 1965:

1965	1,388
1970	940

1975	700
1978	570

But he acknowledged that attendances, particularly at Sunday evening services, had dropped throughout the country, and many churches had no evening service at all.

Father Provincial was exploring the possibility of grant aid for St Mary's, and the Jesuits, with Bishop Alexander's blessing, were determined to stay in the city to continue their mission, but the Trenchard Street premises had been sold (though not the presbytery), and the Social Club already given notice to quit by April 1, 1980. What if the worst were to happen, resulting in no church and no presbytery as such? As the decade drew to an end, Fr Connor looked into the future:

> Surely all we need is a place for worship, Confessions and counselling, and of course living accommodation for the priests. Perhaps during this time of uncertainty we should be thinking about non-church accommodation, bearing in mind the wonderful work being done in the heart of Liverpool where an old cinema has become a busy and thriving spiritual centre. There may not be a cinema available here but there could be business premises, large shops or offices – any place that could be obtained and adapted to our needs without too great an expense provided it is in the city centre and not too far from the Bristol Royal Infirmary. If we had a reasonable target to aim at I think the response from the people of St Mary's would be generous and enthusiastic. Think about it, keep your eyes and ears open for alternative accommodation, and, of course, keep praying.[1]

By now the Society of Jesus had spent tens of thousands of pounds from its own funds on projects to finance the renovation of St Mary's but, just as plan after plan had been rejected, so these had been thwarted and come to nothing. Then all the uncertainties suddenly ended when on Sunday, February 3, 1980, after consultation with the Jesuits, Bishop Alexander announced that St Mary-on-the-Quay was to close and the parish area to be taken over by neighbouring churches.

The closing of a Catholic church like St Mary's was almost without precedent in this country, observed the parish priest: the Jesuits planned to stay in Bristol, but without a parish; they would be engaged in the hospital chaplaincies and the city-centre apostolate.

For many Bristolians to whom the church was a familiar landmark, the news came as a complete surprise. To the shock experienced by parishioners was added the distress of first learning of the closure not from the Bishop at the Sunday Masses, as intended, but hours earlier from the front page of a local newspaper (breaking a press embargo) carrying a picture of St Mary's and the headline: *Famous church closed by rising repair bill.*

Leading members of the congregation, parishioners who had worshipped at St Mary's since childhood and, it would not be too much to say, had worked all their lives for the church, were determined to fight the decision. They addressed a letter setting out the case for retaining St Mary's to the Apostolic Delegate in London, the Most Reverend Bruno Heim, and, having informed the parish priest, sent further copies to Bishop Alexander, Cardinal Hume, and the Father General of the Society of Jesus, Pedro Arrupe in Rome. They expressed their readiness to meet anyone who might be appointed to discuss the matter further.

In the meantime other organisations were left at a loss. Not long before, the Catholic newspaper *The Universe* had carried a special feature on its centre page telling of the dramatic progress of the Association of Our Lady of Mount Carmel and showing a picture of its founder, Margaret Grady, standing by the altar of St Mary-on-the-Quay where eleven years before, on July 16, 1969, in the Upper Hall, the Association was started. Now this world-wide witness of Rosary Circles, thousands of them, in countries such as Canada, Australia, India, South Africa and the United States, was forced to seek other headquarters: "We appeal to anyone in central Bristol to offer a 'home' where we can set up an office for the equipment of the Association and also where meetings may be arranged for the Association's secretariat."

Then, 55 weeks after the first announcement that St Mary's was to close, the decision was made that the church was to be reprieved. Joy and relief greeted this news and, doubtless, no small wonder. "The main reason for saving the church was its value in the city centre as a place of worship and counselling, and of mission to the city," the parish priest explained. But did not the economic arguments compelling closure still hold? Was not the cost of renovation too great? The Bristol Jesuits, it was revealed, had been given an unconditional grant of £100,000 – a way of making good some of the 'deferred maintenance' – towards the £350,000 needed to carry out only essential repairs to the church and to demolish the top and middle halls so that a new presbytery could be built on the vacated site. In addition to the grant the proceeds from the sale of the present presbytery and the Trenchard Street site, together with existing investments, could reduce the shortfall to around £135,000. Surely, it was urged, a realisable target?

There was a new air of optimism – and in the knowledge that every month's delay in commencing building would add £5,000 to the estimated cost, a sense of urgency too. The services of a professional fund-raiser were engaged, and the campaign was given an early boost with an anonymous donation of £20,000. Many projects got under way: for instance two ladies, Sue and Doreen Caple, had 500 Renovation Fund boxes made and distributed and there were responses to their appeal not only from within the city but beyond, from Clevedon, Portishead, and Bath, and even one from Wimbledon. Thousands of pounds were collected in this way.

By May 1981, pneumatic drills and sledgehammers were demolishing the walls of St Joseph's Church, except (by design) the original façade in Trenchard Street, so when the dust and din had subsided and the road was reopened to traffic, the passer-by might well have thought it had all been much ado about nothing: to this day it is as though the first Catholic church to be built in Bristol since the Reformation still stands.

Work at St Mary's had commenced, and was proceeding satisfactorily until it revealed an unexpected problem, the solution to which filled many with dismay.

The church roof above the organ needed repairing, but in order to carry out the necessary work the pipes had to be removed. It was estimated that to do this, and then overhaul and replace them, would cost around £10,000. To resite the pipes in another part of the church, such as the gallery, would cost around £20,000. And throughout the period of renovation St Mary's would, obviously, have no organ.

To save the pipes from damage by dust and falling masonry they were removed, but such was their weight – seven tons in all – it was felt prudent to call in engineers to examine the strength of the gallery before temporarily locating them there. Since the gallery could not safely contain them all, some of the pipes were transferred to the organ works at Taunton for storage, such was now the shortage of space at St Mary's.

It was explained to the congregation that the total cost of dismantling, storing and then replacing the organ in the loft would be £23,062. This would be in addition to the money earmarked for existing renovation work, and to suggest an additional fund-raising effort to meet this new cost would not be realistic. Fr Connor put the problem – and the solution, as he saw it – starkly: We can neither afford to put the organ back in its original position nor can we find a buyer who would also be prepared to meet the necessary cost of installation. We must, therefore, buy an electronic organ within our budget.

Back in 1958 a fund had been set up to rebuild the organ, the cost of which, it was estimated, would be at least £5,000. "There is so much dirt inside the pipes," said one organ specialist, "it is a wonder they play at all." Various means of raising the money were tried, but progress was very slow.

In due course, despite the regrets and misgivings of some, the new organ was duly installed. Time, as we know, is a great healer: later, reporting on an ecumenical service held at the church, the writer observed that afterwards "the admiring crowds around our new organ took some time to disperse."

NOTES

1. *St Mary-on-the-Quay Magazine*, November, 1979.

St Mary's priests, 1993. Relaxing at the presbytery (left to right): Fr
Robert Brooks S.J.; Fr Claudio Rossi S.J. (Parish Priest); Fr Bernard
Charles S.J. (Photo: Bill Joll)

CHAPTER 19

The Mission Continues

The highlight for Catholics in 1982 was the historic visit to Britain of Pope John Paul II. The Pope's Masses at Coventry and Cardiff attracted the largest numbers from the Clifton diocese, though it is likely that the diocese was represented at all the papal events during the unforgettable six days from Friday, May 29 to Wednesday, June 2.

Enthusiasm for the forthcoming visit found expression early on at St Mary's when the congregation was given the opportunity to buy souvenirs in the form of shopping bags at £2.90 and tea towels at £1.50, of which 40p and 20p respectively were for church funds! There was, of course, a more serious, spiritual preparation to be made during the Parish Mission held from March 7 to 10, but the following month the Falklands crisis raised the disturbing question of whether it was a suitable time for the papal visit to take place after all. It was not until little more than two days before the Pope was due to land at Gatwick Airport that it was certain he would make his visit to Britain as planned.

Over 50 people from St Mary's, led by Fr Connor and Fr Bernard McIver, left Temple Meads station by special train half an hour after midnight on Pentecost Sunday for the Pope's Mass at Coventry. Fr McIver recalls the occasion:

We reached Leamington Spa in the small hours of the morning of Whit Sunday. There we were herded into a coach, driven to within a couple of miles of the stadium, and finally left to walk the rest of the way over rough ground and stony tracks. At the end of the pilgrimage we were thankful to find a buffet, seats and hot drinks.

And so to the morning. Those members of the clergy who were not actually concelebrating, vested in albs and stoles to help in the distribution of thousands of communions. Then we were led out and established in a privileged position within fifty yards of the papal altar. Even so, our view of the proceedings was not nearly as good as yours who sat before your television screens. But to be there was the great thing.

And so finally the papal procession made its appearance; representatives of other churches, concelebrating clergy, priests and bishops; and finally Pope John Paul himself, and the Mass commenced. When the time for Holy Communion came, we who were not concelebrating had our own part to play. Bowls of consecrated hosts were brought to us and we were led out to our appointed places [marked by a golden umbrella] to distribute Communion to the vast congregation. It was a strange experience, standing in the middle of a field in the early hours ministering to the crowds as they came streaming up to us.

By the time we had finished the Mass was already over! The remaining hosts were gathered in and we were left to unvest and retrace the rough roads in search of our coaches for our return journey. An exhausting experience, but how very much worth while!

In his homily Pope John Paul spoke of the horrors of warfare – an unacceptable way of settling differences between nations; and he spoke too of Cardinal Newman, "that great man of God, that pilgrim for truth." Concelebrating with him were Cardinal Hume; the Archbishop of Birmingham; Archbishop Heim, the Apostolic Delegate; Bishop Alexander of Clifton; and the Bishops of Shrewsbury and Nottingham. This was the biggest of the rallies held during the six days' visit.

St Mary's parishioners who travelled to the papal service at York[1] racecourse spoke of the holiday atmosphere they found when they reached their destination at 8.30 in the morning: it was a scene of colour, music and tens of thousands of people. The friendliness of the north country people and the entertainment provided ensured that time passed quickly. At noon everything stopped for the Angelus.

The Pope's route was so arranged that everyone was able to see him as he drove through the great throngs before commencing the simple service of prayers and hymns at about 2 o'clock. His homily was devoted to the theme of Marriage and he invited all couples present to renew their marriage vows. The York visit was clearly an occasion of great happiness for all present.

On his final day in Britain, the Pope celebrated Mass at Pontcanna Fields, Cardiff. Again there were worshippers from St Mary-on-the-Quay:

> Our blue entrance tickets had a space for name, address and parish. "Fill them in and then pin them on the children. We learned that from the Irish," said the policeman at the gate.
>
> An altar and graceful canopy on a huge platform in the far distance, a television camera high over the altar, at the side gigantic scaffolding for more cameras, tents in the shade of the trees – excellent organisation and the murmur of Welsh. There were parish banners and the red and white flag denoting his faithful Poles. The black and white flag of Brittany marked a group who had come specially for this Celtic occasion.
>
> Cheers and waving of papal flags as we glimpsed the helicopter and again as the Pope drove around the field. Then the Mass and, despite one's distance from the altar, it seemed an intimate occasion. The Welsh singing and music were unaffected and very moving.
>
> The Pope's theme was the Eucharist and he gave Holy Communion to First Communicants and to their families. Under the famous yellow umbrellas the priests came bearing specially made ciboria. (One was presented to the Pope.) Then he gave his blessing and, suddenly, it was all over.

One of the St Mary's parishioners received an invitation to attend the historic occasion when the Pope and the Archbishop of Canterbury worshipped together at Canterbury Cathdedral: "Luckily there were TV screens in the Cathedral as I did not have the best of views. I saw the Pope's left ear and the back of Prince Charles's head only as they passed in procession! Never mind: I was there and could certainly hear this most moving service. I think what impressed me most was the Pope's clarion call to all of us to seek for truth."

Not since before the Reformation had the Catholic faith in Britain experienced such renewal or such strength as during the visit of Pope John Paul II.

By August 1982, the Renovation Fund had reached £276,236, which included the proceeds from the sale of property and assets. If in addition to the cost of the work still to be completed was added that of redecorating the church (the last major decoration had been 30 years before), it was considered that another £105,000 or more would be needed. But a satisfactory stage in building was soon reached: in December the Fathers moved to their new presbytery next to the church – formerly the site of the old club rooms – so at last fulfilling one of Fr Connor's wishes when he first came to St Mary's.

The repair work continued and, although not completed in all respects (the floor of the crypt was lowered a few months later, with aid from the Manpower Services Commission), it was thought to have advanced sufficiently for the Feast of the Ascension on May 12, 1983 to be also the occasion for marking the renovation of the church. Bishop Alexander celebrated Mass, his co-celebrants being Fr George Earle (Provincial of the Society of Jesus), Fr Tom Connor, Fr Francis Collins and nine other priests. Present in the packed congregation, some of whom had worshipped regularly at the church for 50 years or more, were around 40 Religious Sisters, including representatives of the Sisters of Mercy, who hold a special place in the affections of the St Mary's congregation. It was evident that many people had gone out of their way to pay their own tribute to the church: a special welcome was given to all the non-Catholics present, and to the many former parishioners who had returned to share in celebrating the great Feast of the Ascension and the successful end to the trials of the preceding years.

There was a third cause for celebration: Fr Bernard McIver had been at St Mary's for over 30 years, and the service that evening also honoured his Diamond Jubilee. This self-effacing, dedicated man was born of Catholic parents in Stockport on January 17, 1904. It was during his later years at Stonyhurst, the famous Jesuit college in Lancashire, that he determined to become a priest and he entered the Society of Jesus on September 7, 1922; he was ordained on September 6, 1938. Fr McIver came to Bristol from St Ignatius College, North London, where he had been teaching Classics. He arrived at the presbytery in Trenchard Street ("Where's that?" the taxi driver had asked) on September 29, 1952, and so began his long and dedicated service at St Mary-on-the-Quay.

In those days [he recalled][2] the traffic circulated in front of St Mary's in the reverse direction. All bus services terminated at the Centre, and the buses drew up not at the pavement, but at the central island, round the War Memorial. At the foot of Colston Street there was a scissor-crossing where every vehicle had to cross the route of every other vehicle. The confusion was terrific.

Life, too, has greatly changed. Those were the days when rationing had barely ended after the war, when there were chronic shortages of everything. When I came there were four Masses on Sunday morning at St Mary's, then Evening Service, and that was all. Not for nearly a year was Evening Mass introduced. The effect was beyond belief. On holy days of obligation we had a 5.30 Mass, the only one, at first, in Bristol. Imagine St Mary's packed to the doors, the congregation overflowing into the portico and down the steps. Two other Masses were quickly added, and the other parishes speedily followed suit.

In 1988 Fr McIver celebrated Mass on his 84th birthday: he had served at St Mary's for 36 years.

"Ever since I was an altar-boy they looked, from a distance, like three black blobs." The speaker was referring to the grimy appearance of three large pictures[3] at the back of the gallery before they were removed for cleaning during the general renovation. The large central painting had been damaged while building work was in process and was sent away to be restored; the other two pictures were taken to the sacristy and cleaned. Today from the sanctuary steps they look colourful and striking, and it is surprising to learn that they have little commercial value. The picture of Our Lady is a copy of a painting by the Spanish artist Murillo, and all three are probably the work of Italian artists in the mid-nineteenth century; it is likely that they were hung in the church somewhat later.

Two members of the St Mary's congregation received Bene Merenti medals from Bishop Alexander on November 8, 1983. Vincent Dimambro first served as an altar boy in May 1910 when Fr George Carolan was parish priest. He was born in the parish and married in St Mary's, and his commitment to St Mary's, through various forms of service, was total. He died on August 13, 1991 at the age of 88, by which time he had served on the altar for 81 years.

James Fionda was just 14 and still at school when the then parish priest, Fr Doyle, told him that the organist, Miss Babbage, was away and that he would have to play for Benediction. When Miss Babbage retired he took over the duty of playing for the 9.30 Mass as well, and on the death of Mr Marsh he became the organist at all St Mary's services. He was then 17 years old.

Over the years he has been invited to play at services at Bristol's Colston Hall, Buckfast Abbey, Plymouth Cathedral, Birmingham Town Hall, Westminster's Central Hall, and Manchester's famous church of The Holy Name. Some of the occasions were broadcast. He remains the senior organist at St Mary's.

Both men were born in the St James's area, historically the centre of the Italian community in the city. At the beginning of the century the Italians in the parish numbered around 230 and on special occasions the brightly-coloured costumes of the women presented a picturesque sight in the church. Over the years the service of the community to St Mary-on-the-Quay has been outstanding.

By the end of 1984, with the help of regular fund-raising activities such as the Saturday mini-market, which had been going for just under threee years and had already raised over £11,000, the church was able to meet its commitment to pay £834 monthly to the Society of Jesus, which had lent so much for the renovation of St Mary's. It is interesting that of the original nine helpers when the mini-market was opened on February 6, 1982, five were from St Mary's, one from Holy Cross, one from Clifton Cathedral and two were non-Catholics. Peggy Tudor was succeeded as organiser by Dorothy Tweedie and their good work has been ably continued over the years by Barbara Fox and her loyal band of helpers.

On February 10, 1985 Fr Tom Connor, who had celebrated his Silver Jubilee at St Mary's, left for Osterley Park and was succeeded by Fr William Maher, previously parish priest at Rotherhithe, London. It was Fr Maher who had been so instrumental in saving St Mary's when Provincial of the Society of Jesus.

On August 11, 1987 Fr John Robert Brooks, who had come to St Mary's the previous year, joined the permanent staff. He entered the Society of Jesus on September 7, 1938 and was ordained on September 6, 1952. He then taught at Preston College, where he himself had been educated. He worked with Fr Bernard Bassett[4] for the Christian Life Movement and during the late 60s was Superior at Farm Street, the famous Jesuit church in London. Afterwards he became Superior at Campion House College, Osterley. Later he returned to Lancashire to become parish priest in Blackpool before coming to Bristol. On Sunday, September 6, 1992 he celebrated his Ruby Jubilee.

A month or so before Fr Brooks arrived at St Mary's in 1987 it was decided to sell snacks and lunches daily from the crypt. So was born 'Quay Snacks'.[5] At the end of his lunch-time Masses, Fr Brooks never fails to commend Quay Snacks to his congregation. By his advocacy he must have added greatly to the takings and church funds! Tens of thousands of pounds are raised in selling refreshments, and through Sunday coffee-mornings and Saturday mini-markets, which are weekly events of much longer pedigree.

In mid-1988 Fr Maher, who had energetically committed himself to St Mary's, felt that for health reasons he could no longer give of his best to the parish and suggested to his superiors at Farm Street that they should replace him. At the request of the Provincial he agreed to continue, until November 25th when he took up a new post in Farnborough, and Fr Claudio Rossi, who had joined the staff of St Mary's seven months earlier, became the parish priest.

When Claudio Rossi was a boy in South Africa, living in Port Elizabeth, he asked his father if he could go to St Aidan's, the

Jesuit boarding school in the town of Grahamstown; so began his association with the Society of Jesus. He joined the noviciate in 1972 and was ordained in the church of St Joachim,[6] Rome on October 25, 1975. Fr Rossi afterwards served in what was then Rhodesia for three years before returning to South Africa where he remained for another four years. His next posting was to London, and then after six years in the capital he came to Bristol.

Two events affecting the building occurred in the next few years. In preparation for the 150th anniversary celebration of St Mary's in 1993 the façade of the church was cleaned and floodlighting installed in 1990, somewhat ahead of the celebration date but enabling the parish committee to take advantage of the attractive terms the contractors were able to offer at that time! The other event was unplanned and unwelcome.

At about 5 p.m. on Saturday, February 1, 1992, a young girl driving her car with her companion near the Colston Hall was forced to swerve when another car shot in front of them. The car with its terrified occupants crashed into the front of the presbytery, while a startled Fr Rossi, who at the time was upstairs in his room at the front of the house, felt the building shake and thought that someone had jumped from the adjoining skyscraper and burst through the roof! Fortunately the young girl and her companion were unharmed, apart from some bruising. While the façade of the house was being rebuilt and other necessary repairs made, the front rooms remained uninhabitable. The church office now also served as the parish priest's bedroom, but Fr Rossi willingly accepted the inconvenience, declaring himself well satisfied with the quiet nights he now enjoyed removed from the noise of the busy traffic of Colston Street. The cost of rebuilding, born by the girl's insurers, was over £15,000.

But this is to anticipate a little. In February 1991 Fr John Fairhurst, who had been at St Mary's for just under two years, left to return to St Beuno's College in North Wales (where he had been for a period a few months previously), this time to join the permanent staff helping in retreat and renewal work. He was replaced on April 2 by Fr Bernard Charles.

Fr Charles, an economics and political science graduate from St Andrew's University, joined the Society of Jesus as a novice in February 1970. Six years later he was sent to teach in a seminary in southern Sudan – that war-torn country which has been disrupted by civil strife ever since gaining independence in 1956. He subsequently left for further studies at Sussex University with the aim, approved by his superiors, of returning to the seminary at Wau, but renewed fighting made it almost impossible to get into the country, so after ordination in 1981 he was sent to work with young people in Liverpool's inner city area, based in the Jesuit parish of St Francis Xavier.

There, Fr Charles opened and ran a youth club and as a result was able to do pastoral work with the families of the young people and to help social workers and probation officers in the district. He was later to put his experience of the inner city and its problems at the service of a research institute engaged in the study (on behalf of the government and local authorities) of changes in employment and social life in the postwar housing estates around the fringes of Liverpool. In 1990 he went to El Paso, Texas, and spent six months with an American Jesuit who had built up a number of communities of Hispanic immigrants; it was a period, Fr Charles says, which he found spiritually very fruitful.

At last, at the beginning of 1991, Fr Rossi was able to announce that the church was free from the debt it had incurred over the past decade; thanks to large bequests and the generosity of very many people, it had cleared its indebtedness both to the Society of Jesus and to the Clifton Diocese.

A few months later another happy occasion for St Mary's was the evening of June 14 when two members of the congregation received the papal award, Bene Merenti, from Bishop Alexander.

Alfred Langford had worshipped at St Ignatius church, Stamford Hill in London, from 1947 to 1985 and helped Fr William Maher, the then Rector, to buy an old cinema and rebuild a parish hall on the site. For 21 years he was its manager. He has been an active member of the St Vincent De Paul Society and the Knights of St Columba, and since 1987 manager of St Mary's hall.

As a boy William Joll attended St Mary's School and was an altar server at the church. In addition to assuming other duties at St Mary's he has been head sidesman for about 40 years. His award was also given for his work on behalf of the Little Sisters of the Poor: he was chairman of the Appeals Committee of St Joseph's Home, Bristol.[7]

The following year the papal medal, Pro Ecclesia et Pontifice, was awarded to another member of the congregation, Marion Morgan, not specifically for her work on behalf of St Mary's but for her ecumenical work in Bristol and nationally.

The furtherance of ecumenism is a duty which the Society of Jesus has enjoined upon its members since the decree of the Second Vatican Council, and St Mary-on-the-Quay shares regularly with other city-centre churches in worship and discussion. In the last two years especially, the laity have become more and more involved in the work. The bigotry that marred relationships between Catholic and Protestant in years gone by has disappeared, to be replaced by a spirit of warm and friendly co-operation.

The Society has also called for an increased awareness of the needs of social justice, and in this respect St Mary's, along with other city-centre churches, has supported, with helpers and funds, particularly the work of the Julian Trust and more recently the Little Brothers of Nazareth.[8] The central position of St Mary's ensures that the church is at all times aware of its responsibilities to the less fortunate members of society, and its congregation regards it as a privilege that its church hall is used as the regular weekly meeting place for the organisation of the Handicapped and for Alcoholics Anonymous.

There has already been the successful completion in Zimbabwe of one Mission Outreach project funded by St Mary's donations; since 1989 the church has raised thousands of pounds for five such undertakings overseas – in Zimbabwe, Kenya and Bangladesh.

A hard-working committee provides for the social life of St Mary's. The congregation is greatly appreciative of the regular social occasions and fund-raising events which this committed and dependable group of people organise, much of their work being done quietly in the background.

The most important aspect of life at St Mary's has been the spiritual, all centred on the Mass, the Eucharistic adoration and the Sacrament of Reconciliation, and expressed in a variety of ways – through formal worship, visits, the hospital chaplaincy, and all-night vigils, which are always well attended and attract people from beyond the parish. The laity are actively involved in this devotion which commences at 11 p.m. and ends in the morning with Mass at 7 o'clock.

The hospital chaplaincy has always figured prominently in the work of St Mary's: even if the church had closed in 1980, the Society of Jesus would have ensured that the chaplaincy to the hospital continued. Today it is being undertaken by Fr Bernard Charles, Sisters Dominic and Mary, and members of the laity.

Since 1988, groups from St Mary's, led by the Fathers, have annually visited the great places of pilgrimage in England and abroad – Walsingham, Lourdes, Fatima, Paray-le-Monial and Medjugorje. These journeys of faith are seen by the pilgrims not as spiritual tourism but as times of special grace to deepen their commitment to Christ and His Gospel.

NOTES

1. British Rail at York said passengers were arriving at the rate of 100 a minute.
2. The occasion for these reminiscences had been Fr McIver's Golden Jubilee in 1972: he had then been at St Mary's 20 years. *St Mary-on-the-Quay Magazine*, November, 1972.
3. These were the pictures that Fred O'Connell had cleaned in the 1940s, when he was master of ceremonies at St Mary's.
4. Fr Bernard Basset S.J. wrote *The English Jesuits from Campion to Martindale*, 1967.
5. Before the development of Quay Snacks, 'Fasting Lunches' were available in the crypt every Friday. The contradictory terms were noted at the time by an amused 'Peterborough' in his *Daily Telegraph* column. A useful oxymoron, St Mary's could claim!
6. St Joachim and St Anne were the parents of the Blessed Virgin Mary. The Holy Well of St Anne at Brislington, Bristol, was a famous place of pilgrimage in medieval times. Today, there is an annual procession to the well starting from the local Anglican church of St Anne.
7. At the special Mass to celebrate the 150th anniversary of St Mary-on-the-Quay, held just before the publication of this book,

Michael Ray and Thomas Clements were awarded the papal medal Bene Merenti by the Bishop of Clifton for their loyal service to the church and parish over many years.

8. The Julian Trust and the Little Brothers of Nazareth do splendid work in the city centre on behalf of the homeless and the needy.

The Little Brothers of Nazareth have taken over St James's Church, which is no longer used by the Church of England. It was scarcely 200 yards away that, in about 1743, Fr John Scudamore S.J. set up his chapel in St James's Back. When he died in 1778 he was buried opposite the porch of St James's, but today there is no trace of his grave. The burial register of St James's Church carries the simple entry: "1778, April 11. John Scudamore." Of his priesthood there is no word.

CHAPTER 20

What of the Future?

A photograph of Colston Avenue taken at the end of the nineteenth century shows that today, of all the buildings, only the church of St Mary-on-the-Quay has survived. What of the future? In this 150th anniversary year it is unwise to be too knowing: Edward Irving, whose followers built what was to become St Mary's Church, predicted that the world as we know it would end in 1864 and that Christ would return.

Again, Bishop William Vaughan, who once served the Bristol mission, spoke on July 5, 1890 at the Catholic Truth Society's Conference in Birmingham, and looked 100 years into the future. In his paper on "Prayer for the Conversion of England" he considered that England was already half converted from what she was during the previous three centuries, and that if the progression of change continued, England would be practically Catholic again before the end of the twentieth century. Alas, too many assumptions have to be made and often the hoped-for constants perplexingly become variables: always the unexpected happens.

We know the planning policies of Bristol City Council for the years immediately ahead. A model of the city centre of the future shows the proposed changes to the flow of traffic in Colston Avenue which will affect those visiting St Mary-on-the-Quay: the road in front of St Mary's will be a two-way system used by public transport only, while the road on the far side will be a two-way system for other vehicles. The width of pavement immediately in front of St Mary's will be extended, thus narrowing the road at that point and providing a crossing to the Cenotaph area. Colston Avenue is designated a Key Public Open Space.[1]

There is no reason to suppose that the number of residents in the parish will diminish, unless they deliberately choose to leave. On the contrary – it is now the policy of the City Council to encourage people to live within the centre of the city and there is the likelihood, therefore, of more residential development wherever possible, for example along the waterfront. Housing Priority Areas have been designated.[2]

We may expect the council then to pursue policies for the centre of the city which, among other things, will enhance conservation areas, calm the flow of traffic, and encourage residents to remain.

The role of St Mary-on-the-Quay as parish church and city-centre church fulfilling many needs will continue. Its position in the city is unique. Fr William Maher, former Provincial of the English Province and one-time parish priest at St Mary's, explains: "It has long been the policy of the Jesuits in England to try and place their parish churches as near as possible to the centre of cities. But only here in Bristol has the Order been able to achieve a site which is in every sense central to the heart of the city."

But whatever the future of St Mary-on-the-Quay, we must imitate St Ignatius who once said that if the Society of Jesus collapsed and his life's work was shattered, it would take him a quarter of an hour to recover from the shock, because what mattered was not his reputation but the greater glory of God[3] and the building of his Kingdom. It is for this that those unnamed, loyal and quiet workers of St Mary's and countless other parishes strive. And not in vain – for certain, there will be room and welcome at the end. It was Christ's promise: "In my Father's house are many mansions."

NOTES

1. "Major environmental improvements of the following public spaces will be undertaken aimed at preserving and enhancing their historic identities, upgrading their pedestrian environments and reducing the impact of road traffic: The Centre (Broad Quay) / Colston Avenue / St Augustine's Parade." *Bristol City Centre Draft Local Plan, City Centre Policy Schedule*, April 1992, p.4.
2. "The loss of existing housing will be resisted throughout the Plan area." *Bristol City Centre, Draft Local Plan*, 1990, p.54.

3. Ad maiorem Dei gloriam: the motto of the Society of Jesus.

Priests at St Mary-on-the-Quay

1843 **Fr Patrick O'Farrell O.S.F.**: William Cullinan,
J. Illingworth, William Godwin

1857 **Fr Ferdinand English D. D.**

FATHERS OF THE SOCIETY OF JESUS

1861 **Fr William Johnson**: H. James, Antonio Caradonna,
Vincent Zanetti

1863 **Fr Matthew McCann**: Antonio Caradonna, Peter
Sherlock, Thomas Dykes, Thomas O'Malley

1867 **Fr Thomas Dykes**: Antonio Caradonna, Frederick
Myers, Ignatius Grant, Aloysius Janalik, Alexander
Kyan, J.B. Sangalli, William Kaye, Thomas Meyrick,
Walter Clifford

1873 **Fr Thomas Hill**: Frederick Myers, Walter Clifford,
James Splaine, Gerard Manley Hopkins, Antonio
Caradonna, John Hartell, J. Johnson, Ignatius Grant,
Charles Kerslake, William Strickland, Peter Sherlock

1893 **Fr Thomas Greenan**: John Ross, Joseph O'Gorman,
Walter Clifford, William Edgcome, J. Apel, F. Walsh,
Alfred Hulley

1898 **Fr Thomas Brown**: William Edgcome, Alfred Hulley,
Joseph Reilly, Stanislaus St John

1901 **Fr Francis Grene**: Joseph Reilly, Charles Williams,
George Carolan, Edward Lawless, H. Martyn Parker,
Aloysius Guibarde

1907 **Fr Robert Moss**: H. Martyn Parker, Charles Ruthven,
Alfred Hulley, Frederick Magee, Dominic Lickert

1910 **Fr George Carolan**: Alfred Hulley, Peter McPhillips,
Cuthbert Meyer, Robert Stevenson, Thomas Faulkener,
John Benson

1917 **Fr Joseph Flynn**: Charles Dawson, Richard Hart,

John McGowan

1919 **Fr Michael King**: Richard Hart, Cuthbert Meyer,
Joseph Bamber

1924 **Fr Cuthbert Meyer**: Joseph Bamber, Dominic Lickert,
Oswald Kemball, Theodore Evans, Raymond Mayo,
John Croke, John Brady, Theodore Ellison, John Luck

1934 **Fr Francis Donohoe**: Philip St John, Edmund Sykes,
Joseph Doyle, Joseph Martin, Anthony d'Andria

1938 **Fr Joseph Doyle**: Edmund Sykes, Anthony d'Andria,
Bernard Weatherhead, Bernard Dobson, Thomas Agius,
John Holland

1951 **Fr Lawrence Crehan**: Joseph Taylor, Thomas Smith,
Arthur O'Connor, Bernard McIver, James O'Neill,
Louis Threlfall

1957 **Fr Isaiah Capaldi**: Bernard McIver, James O'Neill,
Louis Threlfall, Francis Lobo, Richard Foley,
Francis Keating, Robert Bulbeck, George Orr,
Leonard Shaw

1963 **Fr Arthur Kavanagh**: Bernard McIver, Robert Bulbeck,
Louis Threlfall, Leonard Shaw, Francis Keating,
Leslie Shields

1968 **Fr Vincent Norbury**: Bernard McIver, Leslie Shields,
Christopher Elliott, Kenneth Nugent, John Edwards,
Andrew Noblet, Henry Waterhouse, William Crooks,
Joseph Stanley, Laurence Lochrie, Raymond Bacon

1977 **Fr Thomas Connor**: Bernard McIver, Henry
Waterhouse, Raymond Bacon, Francis Collins

1986 **Fr William Maher**: Bernard McIver, Francis Collins,
David Fleming, Robert Brooks, William Webb,
Claudio Rossi, Oswald Fishwick

1988 **Fr Claudio Rossi**: Robert Brooks, Oswald Fishwick,
John Fairhurst, Francis Barnett, John Pearson,
Bernard Charles

Note: The names shown are those of the Fathers who, at some time, served
with the Parish Priest during his period of office. The list is not exhaustive:
some priests who served a comparatively short time may have been omitted.

Sources

Most of the material for this book has been drawn from the Jesuit Archives, Mount Street, London; the Clifton Diocesan Archives at St Ambrose House, Bristol, and at the Bristol Record Office; and from St Mary-on-the-Quay parish magazines from 1952 onwards.

BIBLIOGRAPHY

The Jesuits in England by Francis Edwards, 1985

Roman Catholicism in England by Edward Norman, 1985

Collections illustrating the History of the Catholic Religion in the Counties etc. by George Oliver, 1857

Fathers in Faith edited by Aidan Bellenger, 1991

Dr. William Clifford, third Bishop of Clifton (1857-1893): His influence at the First Vatican Council and on the English Catholic Church by J.A. Harding. (Unpublished Ph.D. thesis, University of London, 1991)

Annals of Bristol by John Lattimer, 1893

Government of Bristol 1373-1973 by Elizabeth Ralph

Bristol As It Was (various vols.) by Reece Winstone

Bristol Directories (first published in 1775)

Bristol City Centre Draft Local Plan, February 1990

Bristol City Centre Policy Schedule, April 1992